INVESTMENT POLICY
How to Win the Loser's Game

About the author . . .

Charles D. Ellis is managing partner of Greenwich Associates, the business strategy research and consulting firm. The author of three books and four dozen articles on business, finance and investment management, he is a CFA, has been a Trustee and President of the Institute of Chartered Financial Analysts, and for 20 years an associate editor of the *Financial Analysts Journal.*

Mr. Ellis earned his B.A. at Yale, an M.B.A. (with distinction) at Harvard Business School, where he has twice taught the second-year course in investment management, and his Ph.D. at New York University.

Investment Policy

How to Win the Loser's Game

CHARLES D. ELLIS

Special ICFA Edition

DOW JONES-IRWIN
Homewood, Illinois   60430

This is a special reprint of *Investment Policy: How to Win the Loser's Game*. It was prepared especially for the Institute of Chartered Financial Analysts. This special reprint is not intended for use other than by the Institute of Chartered Financial Analysts. The standard edition of this book can be ordered by contacting Dow Jones-Irwin, 1818 Ridge Road, Homewood, IL 60430. Phone (312) 800-323-4560.

ISBN 1-55623-089-3
Library of Congress Catalog Card No. 85-71879

Printed in the United States of America

6 7 8 9 0 E 2 1 0 9 8 7

For Chad and Harold
who gave me the pleasure
of being Dear Old Dad

"We have striven throughout to guard the student against overemphasis upon the superficial and the temporary . . . this overemphasis is at once the delusion and the nemesis of the world of finance."

Security Analysis—1934 Edition.
Benjamin Graham and David Dodd.

Foreword

Charley Ellis has what I like to see in an author. He is extremely knowledgeable about his subject. He is intellectually provocative. And he serves no one master!

Goodness knows, Ellis is equipped to tell us about investment policy. His client base includes investment managers and clients alike, and he has probably observed the very best and the very worst of both as they approach the delicate policy decisions.

Ellis's "loser's game" thesis has been a challenge to all participants and is integral to this book. Ellis believes that equity markets are efficient because of the combined brainpower, knowledge, and diligence of the information seekers who make crucial investment decisions. I believe the loser's game is magnified by a growing masochism of the investment community—particularly the institutional participants. Let's face it, clients and managers are involved in a self-destructive approach which emphasizes shorter-term performance and encourages turnover of both securities and managers. The timing of such moves and the inherent costs of executing the many changes are powerful forces working against everybody but the conduits for such changes, the brokers and market makers.

Whether it's super efficiency or super masochism, the result is the same. Ellis's answer is not to tell you to buy low and sell high. He starts where we all have to start to eliminate bad habits: at the very beginning. It's "back to fundamentals," which means back to the very reasons why you are investing and what your expectations and scope should be in approaching this. As dull as "policy" may sound, this *is* the starting block!

One thing is certain. If you follow Charley Ellis's philosophy, *you will be different.* Few investors I know form strategies as he recommends. If over 30 years in the investment management business has taught me anything, it is that the biggest and most consistent winners are those who are willing and able to act different from others.

As Ellis implies, this takes fortitude. Like sound philosophies generally, however, once you "believe" and make the step, the path is far less burdensome. This is the lesson to be learned from *Investment Policy*. The frenetic behavior of other investors is creating opportunity. This may be one of the few times when the easy way out may be the most productive. In this fine book, Ellis provides the tools to develop a winner's policy.

Claude N. Rosenberg, Jr.

Preface

A large English oak table dominating the inside left corner of the Morning Room on the ground floor of Boodles', the oldest of the social clubs established more than a century ago in or near St. James's in London, is one of the places in which parts of this book were written. Other locations include hotel rooms in—and airplanes flying between—Johannesburg, San Francisco, Chicago, Nairobi, Princeton, Bermuda, Vail, Boston, New York City, and Atlanta; and of course, at home in Greenwich.

Because my priorities have been my commitments to my family and to the clients of Greenwich Associates, completing this small book has taken a very long time. This long period of gestation has been advantageous to the final result because it has given me the time and opportunity to obtain and incorporate some of the wisdom and knowledge of thoughtful others.

Several friends have given generously of their time and experience in reading and criticizing the various stages of development through which this book has passed on its way to its present form.

Claude N. Rosenberg, Jr., saved it from the oblivion to which it might have been consigned by insisting on a client focus and joshing me out of an inclination toward the stiffness of "academic" writing. Credit for readability belongs to Claude.

Dean LeBaron encouraged me with a delightful mixture of friendly admonition and cheerful *"pourquoi non?"* that must have masked some genuine doubts.

William G. Burns of NYNEX, Karl Van Horn of American Express Asset Management, and Chris Argyris of Harvard all gave me particularly useful comments and raised questions that lead to additions in several key sections that I will always want to claim.

Robert H. Jeffrey gave the kindest compliment by reading each section with the rigor of a Jesuit instructor and offered extensive suggestions on the main theory and on the structure of the argument—and even on choice of words. Any writer would be grateful for the chance to experience such insistent and gracious thinking and editing.

Dero Saunders applied his considerable talents as an editor and instructor in two complete rewritings. I now know why he expects to be remembered as the editor who could remove four lines from the Lord's Prayer without anyone noticing.

Susan Ellis, as she has done so many times before, used her clarity of mind to bring order and consistency to the language and strength to the exposition.

Lucy Carino, Ann Del Grande, Jeanne Gans, Sandy Jones, and Debra Jo Pennell, all members of Greenwich Associates, typed and retyped the all too numerous drafts through which the final text "evolved."

Special thanks are due to dozens of senior investment professionals who have participated in a series of three-day seminars on investment policy and practice—sponsored by my friends and former partners at Donaldson, Lufkin, and Jenrette—which it has been my great privilege to lead for nearly 20 years. Many of the ideas in the book have been developed at these seminars.

Finally, I wish to recognize explicitly my admiration and respect for the large number of extraordinarily talented, resourceful, and hardworking men and women who compete for success at our nation's investing institutions and securities firms. It is a profound but ironic compliment that their skillful striving is what has made it possible to propose the approach advocated in this book to investment policy.

Charles D. Ellis

Contents

1

Do Clients Matter?

After you read this book, you will know all you will ever need to know to be truly successful with investments.

For such a small book, this ambition may seem far too bold. But there is a countervailing modesty.

This book does not intend to explain how to be successful at traditional investment management—how to pick stocks, time markets, or execute major strategic shifts in a portfolio. Such a treatise would certainly require far greater length. It would be written for professional investment managers as producers and sellers of investment services. And it would be based on the assumption that it is feasible to outperform other investors in the active-aggressive kind of investment management that dominates institutional investing today. This basic assumption must now be in question[1]—only because so many talented, informed, experienced, and diligent professionals are working so hard at institutional investing that they make it unrealistic for any one manager to outperform these other professionals.

This book is different. Far from accepting the conventional wisdom that talented, competitive, professional investment man-

---

[1] Fifteen years ago when I was writing *Institutional Investing* (also published by Dow Jones-Irwin) it made sense to prescribe and advocate a strategic approach to active management. Today, the world of investment management is different, and the time has come for a different concept of the problem of investing and an appropriately different concept of the solution.

1

agers can beat the market, it questions closely the whole concept of institutional investing as it is practiced today.

This book is not written for the sellers of investment management services. It is written for the buyers who, as clients of
professional investment managers, have a real responsibility to
themselves to understand the basic nature of institutional investing, why investment managers succeed or fail, and what can
be done to achieve long-term investment success, even when
their professional investment managers are failing to beat the
market.

This consumers guide to investment management is designed to meet the needs of the many individual investors who
entrust their family savings to mutual funds, trust companies,
and investment advisors; the needs of the corporate executives,
union, and public officials responsible for pension funds; and the
needs of the men and women who serve as trustees of the endowments of universities, museums, schools, hospitals, and
foundations.

This book is written with a clear point of view; clients of
investment managers all too often delegate or more accurately
abdicate to their investment managers responsibilities which they
can and should keep for themselves. Their undelegatable responsibilities are: setting explicit investment policies consistent
with their objectives, defining long-range objectives which are
appropriate to their particular fund, and managing their managers to ensure that their policies are being followed.

This book is a guide for those who will accept this central
client responsibility and who want to be active, responsible, and
successful; whether as fiduciaries or for their own account.

Much as it might seem obvious that client investors should
care a lot about the way their money is managed, the reality is
they typically do almost nothing about it—until it's too late.

Despite the fact that everybody "knows" that each family
fortune or pension fund or endowment fund differs in situation
from every other fund (and that these differences are often quite
substantial), and despite the conventional consensus that these
substantial differences should be reflected in different investment policies and practices, the plain fact is that the investment
portfolios of most funds are very much alike.

This is not the way it should be. The needs and purposes
of the funds are not the same and their investment portfolios
should not be the same.

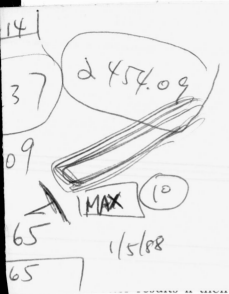

n is a powerful phenomenon in phys-
investments.

n from their clients, it is natural for
1ove toward the center, to put port-
nventional. (It is also easier to treat
ther words, investment managers will
portfolios for *all* their clients rather
efully designed to meet the particular
1al client.

nically, professional investment man-
r again that they feel they must com-
decisions because clients do not do
managers believe they could achieve
clients took a longer-term view of the
investment process and if their clients would only be more specific about the kind of investment portfolio they really want.

Clients "own" the central responsibility for formulating and
assuring implementation of long-term investment policy. As has
been suggested and will be shown, this responsibility cannot be
delegated to investment managers. Fortunately, this client responsibility can be fulfilled without extensive experience in securities analysis or portfolio management.

To fulfill their responsibilities to themselves, clients need three
characteristics: (1) a genuine interest in developing an understanding of their own true interests and objectives, (2) an appreciation of the fundamental nature of capital markets and investments, and (3) the discipline to work out the basic policies
that will, over time, succeed in achieving their realistic investment objectives. That's what this book is about.

Investment managers will also find this book useful in providing a context for the work to which they devote so much of
their time and skill—the day-to-day management of investment
portfolios. Managers should encourage their clients to use this
book as a guide to performing the vital role of being informed,
active, and *successful* clients.

While it is a spirited critique of contemporary practice in
institutional investing, this book is by no means a condemnation
of investment managers. The problem is not that professional
managers lack skill or diligence. Quite the opposite. The problem with trying to beat the market is that professional investors
are so talented, so numerous, and so dedicated to their work
that as a group they make it very difficult for any one of their

number to do significantly better than the others, particularly in the long run.

There are two different kinds of problems in trying to beat the market. One problem is that it is so very difficult to do—and so easy, while trying to do better, to do *worse*. The other problem with targeting on beating the market as a primary investment objective is that this focus diverts the attention of both the investment manager and the client from the need to establish long-range objectives and investment policies that are well matched to the particular needs of the individual client. The real purpose of investment management is not to "beat the market," but to do what is really right for a particular client. And making sure the manager concentrates on achieving that objective is the responsibility of the client.

Does the client matter? Indeed he *should.* But the client will only matter if he asserts his authority and fulfills his responsibility: deciding investment objectives, developing sound investment policies, and holding portfolio managers accountable for implementing long-term investment policy in daily portfolio operations.

2

The Loser's Game

Disagreeable data are steadily streaming out of the computers of the performance measurement firms. Over and over again, these facts and figures inform us that investment managers are failing to "perform." Occasional periods of above average results raise expectations that are soon dashed as false hopes. Contrary to their often articulated goal of outperforming the market averages, the nation's investment managers are not beating the market; the market is beating them.

Faced with information that contradicts what they believe, humans tend to respond in one of two ways. Some will ignore the new knowledge and hold to their former beliefs. Others will accept the validity of the new information, factor it into their perception of reality, and then put it to use.

Investment management, as traditionally practiced, is based on a single basic belief: Professional investment managers *can* beat the market. That premise appears to be false, particularly for the very large institutions that manage most of the assets of most trusts, pension funds, and endowments, because their institutions have effectively become the market.

If the premise that it is feasible to outperform the market were acceptable, then deciding *how* to go about achieving success would be a matter of straightforward logic.

First, since the overall market can be represented by a passive and public listing such as the Standard & Poor's 500 Stock

5

Index, the successful manager need only rearrange his portfolios more productively than the "mindless" S&P 500. He can be different in stock selection, or strategic emphasis on particular groups of stocks, or market timing, or in various combinations of these.

Second, since the active manager will want to make as many "right" decisions as possible, he will assemble a group of bright, well-educated, highly motivated, hardworking professionals whose collective purpose will be to identify underpriced securities to buy and overpriced securities to sell—and to beat the market by shrewdly "betting against the house."

Unhappily, the basic assumption that most institutional investors can outperform the market is not true. The institutions *are* the market. They cannot, as a group, outperform themselves. In fact, given the cost of active management—fees, commissions, and so forth—most large institutional investors will, over the long term, underperform the overall market.

Because investing institutions are so numerous and capable and determined to do well for their clients, investment management is not a winner's game. It is a loser's game.

Before analyzing what happened to convert institutional investing from a winner's game to a loser's game, consider the profound difference between these two kinds of games. In a winner's game, the outcome is determined by the winning actions of the *winner*. In a loser's game, the outcome is determined by the losing behavior of the *loser*. The conceptual distinction can be made entertaining by quoting an eminent scientist, a distinguished historian, and a renowned educator. They are, respectively, Dr. Simon Ramo of TRW; naval historian Admiral Samuel Elliot Morison; and professional golf instructor Tommy Armour.

Simon Ramo identified the crucial difference between a winner's game and a loser's game in his excellent book on playing strategy, *Extraordinary Tennis for the Ordinary Tennis Player*.[1] Over a period of many years, Dr. Ramo observed that tennis was not one game, but two—one played by professionals and a very few gifted amateurs; the other played by all the rest of us.

Although players in both games use the same equipment, dress, rules and scoring, and conform to the same etiquette and customs, the basic natures of their two games are quite differ-

---

[1]Simon Ramo, *Extraordinary Tennis for the Ordinary Tennis Player* (New York: Crown Publishers, 1977).

ent. After extensive scientific and statistical analysis, Dr. Ramo summed it up this way: Professionals *win* points; amateurs *lose* points.

In expert tennis, the ultimate outcome is determined by the actions of the winner. Professional tennis players stroke the ball with strong, well-aimed shots, through long and often exciting rallies, until one player is able to force an error by his opponent or drive the ball just out of reach. These splendid players seldom make mistakes.

Amateur tennis, Dr. Ramo found, is almost entirely different. Brilliant shots, long and exciting rallies, and seemingly miraculous recoveries are few and far between. On the other hand, the ball is fairly often hit into the net or out of bounds, and double faults at service are not uncommon. The amateur duffer seldom beats his *opponent,* but he beats *himself* all the time. The victor in this game of tennis gets a higher score *because his opponent is losing even more points.*

As a scientist and statistician, Dr. Ramo gathered data to test his hypothesis in a clever way. Instead of keeping conventional game scores—love, 15 all, 30–15, and so forth—Ramo simply counted points won versus points lost. He found that in expert tennis about 80 percent of the points are won, but in amateur tennis about 80 percent of the points are lost.

The two games are, in their fundamental characteristic, opposites. Professional tennis is a winner's game whose outcome is determined by the activities of the winner. In amateur tennis, the final outcome is determined by the activities of the loser— who defeats himself. It's a loser's game.

Switching from tennis to military science, Admiral Samuel Elliot Morison makes a similar central point in his thoughtful treatise *Strategy and Compromise:* "In warfare, mistakes are inevitable. Military decisions are based on estimates of the enemy's strengths and intentions that are usually faulty, and on intelligence that is never complete and often misleading." (Doesn't this sound like investment management?) "Other things being equal," concludes Morison, "the side that makes the fewest strategic errors wins the war."[2]

War is the ultimate loser's game. Golf is another. Tommy Armour, in his great book *How to Play Your Best Golf All the*

---

[2]Samuel Elliot Morison, *Strategy and Compromise.*

Time, says: "The best way to win is by making fewer bad shots,"[3] an observation with which all weekend golfers would concur. There are many other loser's games. Some, like institutional investing, were once winner's games, but have changed into loser's games with the passage of time. For example, 60 or 70 years ago only very brave, athletic, strong-willed young people with good eyesight had the nerve to try flying an airplane. In those glorious days, flying was a winner's game. But times have changed and so has flying. If the pilot of your 747 came aboard today wearing a 50-mission hat with a long, white silk scarf around his neck, you'd get off. Such people no longer belong in airplanes because flying today is a loser's game with one simple rule: Don't make mistakes.

These examples should suffice to prove that the requisite player strategy is very different for the two kinds of games, and to show that winner's games can and sometimes do become loser's games.[4] That is what has happened to the "money game" we call investment management.

A basic change has occurred in the investment environment; the market came to be dominated in the 1970s by the very institutions that were striving to win by outperforming the market. In just 10 years, the market activities of the investing institutions shifted from only 30 percent of total public transactions to an overwhelming 80 percent. And that shift made all the difference. No longer was the active investment manager competing with cautious custodians or amateurs who were out of touch with the market: Now he was competing with other experts.

The money game includes a formidable group of competitors. At least 200 major institutional investors and another 1,000 small- and medium-sized institutions operate in the market all day, every day, in the most intensely competitive way.

The key question under the new rules of the game is this: How much better must the active manager be to *at least* recover the costs of active management? The answer is daunting. If we assume 30 percent portfolio turnover (which is lower than the institutional average) and total transaction costs (commission plus the spread between the bid and the ask side of the market

---

[3]Tommy Armour, *How to Play Your Best Golf All the Time* (New York: Simon & Schuster, 1971).

[4]Perhaps winner's games self-destruct because they attract too many players—all of whom want to win. (That's why gold rushes finish ugly.)

including occasions when large blocks of stock are being bought or sold in distress) of 2 percent to buy and 2 percent to sell (certainly not high estimates), plus a fee for active management of 0.4 percent (which is increasingly "normal"), the actively managed portfolio's operating costs are 1.6 percent per annum.[5]

Recovering these costs is surprisingly difficult. For example, assuming an average annual rate of return of 15 percent for equities, of which six percent is the equity premium return (i.e., about the way it has been for the past 50 years), then the active manager must recover the 1.6 percent annual operating costs by increasing the 6 percent equity premium return by more than 25 percent.[6]

Such superior performance can be done and is done every year by some institutions, but it has not been done consistently over a long period of time by many.

The stark reality is that most money managers have been losing the money game. The historical record is that in the 15 years ending with 1984, on a cumulative basis, nearly three quarters of professionally managed funds underperformed the S&P 500 Market Stock Average.

That being true, the burden of proof is on the person who says, "I am a winner, I can win the money game." Because only a sucker backs a "winner" in a loser's game, prospective clients have a right to demand that the investment manager explain exactly what he or she is going to do and why it is going to work so very well.

If investment managers are on balance not beating the market, then they certainly should at least consider joining it. The data from the performance measurement firms suggest that a market fund (i.e., an index fund) would have outperformed most investment managers over long periods of time.

---

[5](0.4 percent + .3 × [2 percent + 2 percent]). Far more than brokerage commissions and dealer spreads are properly included in transactions costs. The best way to show how large transactions costs really are is to compare the *theoretical* results of a "paper portfolio" with the *actual* results of a "real money portfolio." Experts will tell you the differences are always impressive. And there's yet another cost of transactions—the cost of unwisely getting into stocks you would not have attempted if you were not "sure" you could get out at any time because the market looks so liquid. This is a real liquidity trap. Think how differently people would behave on the highway or in the bedroom if they were not so sure they'd not be caught. It's the same way in investments: you don't always get caught nor do you always *not* get caught. *All* of these costs are part of the *total transactions costs*.

[6]26.7 percent to be exact.

The reason that institutional investing has become a loser's game is that in the complex problem each manager is trying to solve, his efforts, and the efforts of his many determined competitors, to find a solution have become the dominant variables. And their efforts to beat the market are no longer the most important part of the solution; they are the most important part of the problem. So many professional investment managers are so good, they make it nearly impossible for any one to outperform the market they now dominate.

The beginning of wisdom for clients of investment managers is to understand why so few—if any—major investment organizations can or will outperform the market averages over long periods of time and how very difficult it is to estimate which managers will outperform.

The next step would be to decide whether—even if it could be won—this loser's game is a game worth playing.

3

Beating the Market

The only way to beat the market, after adjusting for market risk, is to discover and exploit other investors' mistakes.

It can be done. And it has been done by most investors some of the time. But very few investors have been able to outsmart and outmaneuver other investors enough to beat the market consistently over the long term.

Active investment managers can work on any or all of four investment vectors:

1. Market timing.
2. Selection of specific stocks or groups of stocks.
3. Changes in portfolio structure or strategy.
4. An insightful, long term investment concept or philosophy.

Even the most casual observer of markets and securities will be impressed by the simply splendid array of apparent opportunities to do better than "settle for average." The price charts for the overall market, for major industry groups, and for individual stocks make it seem obvious that active investors can and should do better.

MARKET TIMING

The most audacious way to increase potential returns is market timing. The classic market timer moves the portfolio in and out

11

of the market so it is, he hopes, fully invested during rising markets and out of the market when prices are falling. Another form of timing would shift an equity portfolio out of stock groups that are expected to underperform the market and into groups that may outperform the market.

In a bond portfolio the market timer hopes to shift into long maturities before falling interest rates drive up long bond prices, and back into short maturities before rising interest rates drive long bond prices down.

In a balanced portfolio the market timer strives to invest more heavily into stocks when they will produce greater total returns than bonds, then shift into bonds when they will produce greater total returns than equities, and into short-term investments when they can produce greater total returns than either bonds or stocks.

A delightful comparative analysis of two kinds of investment perfection for the period 1940–73 gives a sense of the seductive "potential" of market timing. The first record was the result of perfect market timing with 100 percent in equities in all rising markets and 100 percent in cash in all falling markets.

With 22 transactions (11 buys and 11 sells) in 34 years, and using the Dow Jones Industrial Average as a proxy for equities, $1,000 was expanded into $85,937.

During the same 34-year period, with the hypothetical portfolio always 100 percent invested and always invested in the one best industry group, the same $1,000 (with 28 buys and 28 sells) exploded into $4,357,000,000! The last two years indicate the pluck requisite to the process: In January 1971, $687 million was invested in restaurant companies and became $1.7 billion by year end, and was then committed to gold stocks which carried it up to $4.4 billion by Christmas! Of course this example is absurd. It has never been done and never will be done. More importantly, even far less magical results have not and will not be achieved through "timing" because no one manager is so much more astute than his or her competitors.

Despite the enticing appeal of reducing market exposure by astute sales when securities appear to be overpriced, and boldly reinvesting when prices appear to have declined to attractive low levels—selling high and buying low—the overwhelming evidence shows that market timing is not an effective way to increase returns for one dour but compelling reason: on average and over time, *it does not work.*

The evidence on investment managers' success with market timing is impressive—and overwhelmingly negative. One careful study of market timing concluded that an investment manager would have to be right on his market forecast 75 percent of the time for his portfolio just to *break even* after measuring the costs of mistakes and the costs of transactions. Robert Jeffrey has explained why it is so difficult to improve results with market timing: so much of the "action" occurs in such brief periods and at times when investors are most likely to be captives of a conventional consensus. An unpublished study of 100 large pension funds and their experience with market timing found that while all the funds had engaged in at least some market timing, not one of the funds had improved its rate of return as a result of its efforts at timing. In fact, 89 of the 100 lost as a result of "timing"—and their losses averaged a daunting 4.5 percent over the five-year period.

As MIT's Professor Fischer Black puts it, "The market does just as well, on average, when the investor is *out* of the market as it does when he is *in*. So he loses money, relative to a simple buy-and-hold strategy, by being out of the market part of the time."

Perhaps the best insight into the difficulties in market timing came from an experienced professional's candid lament: "I've seen lots of interesting approaches to market timing—and I have tried most of them in my 40 years of investing. They may have been great before my time, but not one of them worked for me. Not one!"

There is no evidence of any large institutions having anything like consistent ability to get in when the market is low and get out when the market is high. Attempts to switch between stocks and bonds, or between stock and cash, in anticipation of market moves, have been unsuccessful much more often than they have been successful.

STOCK SELECTION

The second tactical way to increase returns is through stock selection or "stock picking." Professional investors devote an extraordinary amount of skill, time, and effort to this work. Stock pricing dominates the research efforts of investing institutions and the research services of stock brokers.

Through financial analysis or field studies of competitors and suppliers as well as management interviews, investors seek to attain a better understanding of the investment value of a security or group of securities than the market consensus. When investment managers find significant differences between the price and the value of a security (as they appraise it), they can buy or sell, as appropriate, to capture the differential between the market's price and the true investment value for their clients' portfolios.

Unfortunately, however, security analysis does not appear to be a useful or profitable activity. The stock investment managers sell after doing fundamental research, and the stocks they don't buy, typically do as well as the stocks they do buy.

Again, the problem is not that investment research is not done well. The problem is that it is done so very well by so many that no one group of investors is likely to gain a regular useful advantage over all other investors.

PORTFOLIO STRATEGY

Strategic decisions—in both stock and bond portfolios—involve major commitments that affect the overall structure of the portfolio. They are made to exploit insights into major industry groups or changes in the economy and interest rates or anticipated shifts in the valuation of major types of stocks such as "emerging growth" stocks or "basic industry" stocks. Each of these judgments would involve what can be described as market segment risk.

For example, in 1980 portfolio managers who invested heavily in two areas—oil and technology—had very favorable results compared to investors who chose instead to invest heavily in utilities and other interest-sensitive stocks or in consumer stocks. Equally important, they had to be out of energy stocks in 1981 or they would "give it all back."

In the early 1970s, portfolio managers who invested heavily in large capitalization growth stocks—the "nifty 50"—experienced exceptionally favorable results as the notorious "two tier" market developed.[1] In the later 1970s, large positions in these same securities produced exceptionally negative market results when previously anticipated earnings failed to materialize and

---

[1]Growth stocks had a much higher P/E ratio than industrial stocks, dividing the market into two tiers.

institutions became disenchanted with the concept and dumped their holdings which collapsed the price/earnings (P/E) ratios and brought stock prices way down. The same sort of thing happened with small high tech stocks in the 1980s, appreciating far faster than the market from 1980 to 1983 and then falling much faster than the market in 1984.

As the well-worn saying goes, it is not a stock market but a market of stocks—one that invites portfolio managers (but not without peril) to make major strategic decisions on groups of stocks in the portfolios they manage.

Full of interesting potential—being in the right place at the right time—this approach to investing challenges the manager to discover the new (and often unfamiliar) way to invest as markets shift, become proficient at each new way, and then abandon it for another new way. Of course, it can be done, but will it be done? By which managers? For how long?

INVESTMENT PHILOSOPHY

The fourth possible means to increase returns is to develop a profound and valid insight into the forces that drive a particular sector of the market or a particular group of companies or industries and systematically exploit that investment insight or concept.

Investing to exploit an investment concept or philosophy involves an enduring investment commitment—through cycle after cycle in the stock market and in the business economy—for an individual portfolio manager or an entire investment management organization.

An organization that is committed, for example, to growth stock investing will concentrate on evaluating new technologies, understanding the management skills required to lead rapidly growing organizations, analyzing the financial requirements of investing in new markets and new products to sustain growth. This investment organization will, it is hoped, learn from experience—no doubt sometimes painful experience—how to discriminate between ersatz "growth stocks" that fizzle out and true growth companies that will achieve success over many years.

Other investment management organizations take the view that among the many large corporations in mature and often cyclical industries, there are always some that have considerably greater investment value than is recognized by other investors;

that with an astute research capability these superior values can be isolated; and that by buying good values at depressed prices they can achieve superior returns for their clients with relatively low risk. Such organizations will develop considerable expertise in "separating the wheat from the chaff," avoiding the low-priced stocks that *ought* to be low priced, and ferreting out insights into investment value that other investors have not yet recognized.

Among the variety of different concepts of investing that can be pursued over many, many years, one emphasizes medium-sized growth companies in specialized industries while another focuses on assets rather than earnings with confidence that carefully chosen, well-positioned assets can and will some day be redeployed to earn good profits. Another group of "contrary opinion" investors will concentrate on stocks that are clearly out of favor with most investors, confident that by looking where prices are depressed, and analyzing many companies dispassionately, they will find bargains.

The important test of an investment concept or philosophy is the manager's ability to adhere to it for valid, long-term reasons—even when the short-term results are most disagreeable and disheartening. Persistence can lead to mastery and development of an important distinctive competence in the particular kind of investing in which the manager specializes.

The great advantage to the concept or philosophical approach is that the investment firm can organize itself to do its own particular kind of investing all the time, avoid the noise and confusion of alternatives, attract investment analysts and managers interested in and skilled at the particular type of investing, and through continuous practice, self-critique, and study to master it. The great disadvantage is that if the chosen kind of investing becomes obsolete or out of touch with the changing market, a proficient specialist organization is most unlikely to detect the need for change until it is too late.

What is remarkable about these profound investment concepts is how few have been discovered that last for very long—most likely because the hallmark of a free capital market is that few if any opportunities to establish a proprietary long-term competitive advantage can be found and maintained for a long time.

All four of these basic forms of active investing have one fundamental characteristic in common: *They depend upon the errors of others.* Whether by omission or commission, the only way in which a profit opportunity can be available to the active investor—in an individual stock or a group of stocks—is that the consensus of other investors is *wrong*.

With so many competitors seeking superior insight into the value/price relationship of individual stocks or industry groups, and with so much information so widely and rapidly communicated throughout the investment community, the chances of discovering and exploiting profitable insights into individual stocks or groups of stocks—opportunities left behind by the errors and inattention of other investors—are certainly not richly promising.

With so many apparent opportunities to do better than the market, it must be disconcerting for investment managers—and their clients—to see how hard it is for investment managers, in fact, to do better than the market after adjustment for risk[2] over the long haul. Yet, even the most talented investment manager must wonder how he can expect his hardworking and determined competitors to provide him—through incompetence, error, or inattention—with sufficiently attractive opportunities to buy or sell in size on significantly advantageous terms on a regular basis so he can "beat the market."

---

[2]See Chapter 2 for an explanation.

4

The Powerful Plodder

The largest part of any portfolio's total long-term returns will come from the simplest investment decision that can be made, and by far the easiest to implement: buying the market.

Hopelessly unpopular with investment managers and with most clients, the uninspiring, dull "market portfolio" is seldom given anything like the respect it deserves.

Plodding along in its unimaginative, inexpensive, "no brain" way, this "plain Jane" form of investing will, over time, achieve better results than most professional investment managers.

Active investment managers—particularly those with good records—accept the proposition that the market portfolio achieves good long-term returns, but they see an opportunity and challenge to do better. "Even 1 percent on a $100 million or $500 million portfolio is a lot of money—particularly when it's 1 percent compounded year after year—and well worth going after."

They may be right. Some *will* be right. But clients should know that they won't *all* be right. Indeed, the evidence so far is that a great majority of managers will not. Their clients would have done better in a market fund.[1]

---

[1] One caution is important regarding "market" funds. Significant sectors are left out of the traditional market indexes. Some of the most interesting and rewarding areas of investing in the past decade—particularly small company stocks—are either not included in the index or are underrepresented. And all the international markets—more than half of the world market—are not included. To compensate for these gaps, new "extended" market funds are being designed to capture the "whole" market.

Considering the time, cost, and effort devoted to achieving better than market results, the market fund certainly produces a lot for a little. This dull workhorse portfolio may appear virtually mindless, but is, in fact, based on an extensive body of research about markets and investments that is well worth examining and can be summarized briefly.

To summarize, the securities market is an open, free, and competitive market in which large numbers of well informed and price-sensitive investors and professional investment managers compete skillfully, vigorously, and continuously as both buyers and sellers. Nonexperts can easily retain the services of experts. Prices are quoted widely and promptly. Effective prohibitions against market manipulations are established. And arbitrageurs, traders, market technicians, and longer-term "fundamental" investors seek to find and profit from any market imperfections. Such a market is considered "efficient."[2] In an efficient market, changes in prices will follow the pattern described as a "random walk," which means even close observers of the market—"tape readers"—will not be able to find patterns in securities prices with which to predict future price changes on which they can make profits.

Moreover, because other competing investors are well-informed buyers and sellers, particularly when they are considered in the aggregate, it will be unlikely that any one investment manager can regularly obtain profit increments for a large portfolio through fundamental research. The more you believe the market is efficient, the more you will believe the rule that the more numerous the skillful competitors, the less likely anyone will achieve consistently superior results.

In a perfectly efficient market, prices not only reflect any information that could be inferred from the historical sequence of prices, but also incorporate and impound all that is knowable[3] about the companies whose stocks are being traded. An efficient market does not mean that stocks will always sell at the "right" price. Investors can be quite *wrong* in their judgments—overly

---

[2] Not perfect, and not even perfectly efficient, but sufficiently efficient that wise investors will not expect to be able to exploit its inefficiencies regularly.

[3] While there is some specialized evidence that quarterly earnings reports and information on "insider transactions" are not immediately and completely discounted in securities prices, the apparent opportunities to be exploited are so very limited that managers of large portfolios would not be able to make effective use of this kind of information anyway.

optimistic, overly pessimistic—and this will show up in later changes in prices. A market can be quite clumsy on valuations and still be very efficient on market information and on fundamental information about companies. (That's why the best opportunities for active investment managers to add value may well come from being wiser and less susceptible to the psychology of the crowd than others.)

The market fund provides investment managers and their clients with an easy alternative. They do not have to play the more complex games of equity investing unless they *want* to play.

This is a marvelous freedom of choice. The option to use the market fund enables any investment manager always to keep pace with the market virtually without effort. It allows the investor to play only when and where and only for so long as he really wants to—and to select any part of the wide investment spectrum for deliberate action at any time for as long or as brief a period as he wishes.

Even for the most self-assured and capable investment managers, the ability to call "time out" and to invest at any time in a market fund is an important advantage because superior knowledge and skill are not consistent attributes of investment managers. Superior knowledge is a *variable*. This freedom not to play carries the reciprocal responsibility to play only for cause, and only when the incremental reward fully justifies the incremental risk.

Investment managers and their clients would be wise to devote more attention to understanding the real advantages offered by the market fund—the powerful plodder.

5

The Paradox

A paradox is haunting investment management.

The paradox is that funds with very long-term purposes are being managed to meet short-term objectives that may be neither feasible nor important. And they are *not* being managed to achieve long-term objectives that are both feasible and worthwhile.

The unimportant and difficult task to which most investment managers devote most of their time with little or no success is trying to "beat the market." Realistically—without taking above-average market risk—to outperform the equity market by even one half of 1 percent *consistently* would be a great success which almost no sizable investment managers have achieved for very long.

The truly important but not very difficult task to which investment managers and their clients could and should devote themselves involves four steps: (1) understanding the client's needs, (2) defining realistic investment objectives that can meet the client's needs, (3) establishing the right asset mix for each particular portfolio, and (4) developing well-reasoned, sensible investment policies designed to achieve the client's realistic and specified long-term investment objectives. In this work, success can be easily achieved.

For example, if the long-term average rate of return on bonds is 8 percent, and the return from investments in common stocks is 16 percent—because there must be a higher long-term rate of return on stocks to convince investors to accept the risk of equity investing—then shifting just 5 percent of the portfolio's assets from bonds to stocks and keeping it there would, over time, increase the portfolio's average annual rate of return by $^4/_{10}$ of 1 percent (8 percent × 5 percent = 0.40 percent).

Shifting the asset mix of a 60 percent equity/40 percent fixed income portfolio to 65:35 is not a major proposition, but, as noted in the previous chapter, consistently beating the market rate of return by 40 basis points a year through superior stock selection would be a substantial achievement.

Very few institutional investors have been able to achieve and sustain such superior results.

It is ironic that a change of even such modest magnitude in the basic asset allocation decision can capture an improvement in total return significantly greater than the elusive increment sought in the beat the market syndrome.

Clearly, if the asset mix truly appropriate to the client's objectives justified an even more substantial emphasis equities— 70:30, or 80:20, or 90:10, or even 100:0—the incremental rate of return, on average, over the 60:40 portfolio would be even greater: 0.8 percent annually at 70:30 increasing to 1.6 percent annually at 80:20 and 3.2 percent average annually at 100 percent. Virtually no substantial investment manager can hope to beat the market by such magnitudes.

Of course, these calculations are mechanical. They present averages ignoring the fact that actual returns in individual years come in an impressive, even intimidating, distribution around these averages.

The crucial question is not simply whether long-term returns on common stocks would exceed returns on bonds or bills *if* the investor held on through the many startling gyrations of the market.

The crucial question is whether the investor will, in fact, hold on. The problem is not in the market, but in ourselves, our perceptions, and our reactions to our perceptions. This is why it is so important for each client to develop a realistic knowledge of his own and/or his organization's tolerance for market fluctuations and his long-term investment objectives, and to develop a realistic understanding of investing and of capital markets. The more you know about yourself as an investor and the more you understand investment management and the securities markets, the more you will know what asset mix is really right for your portfolios, and the more likely you will be able to sustain your commitment for the long term.

In investment management, the real opportunity to achieve

superior results is not in scrambling to outperform the market, but in establishing *and adhering to* appropriate investment policies over the long term—policies that position the portfolio to benefit from riding with the main long-term forces in the market. Investment policy, wisely formulated by realistic and well-informed clients with a long-term perspective and clearly defined objectives, is the foundation upon which portfolios should be constructed and managed over time and through market cycles.

In reality, very few investors have developed such investment policies. And because they have not, most investment managers are left to manage their clients' portfolios without knowing their clients' real objectives and without the discipline of explicit agreement on their mission as investment managers. *This is the client's fault.*

As a result of not knowing enough about the particular facts and values of their different clients, investment managers typically manage all funds in virtually the same way and with very nearly the same asset mix, even in such extraordinarily different kinds of employee benefit funds as pension funds and profit sharing funds.

The profound differences between the functions and needs of pension plans and profit sharing plans make them striking examples of a disconcertingly standardized approach to the most important investment decision: the asset mix. So far as the total sum received by each individual is concerned, profit sharing plans terminate entirely on the day he or she retires or leaves; thus the fund has a series of absolute and predictable end points.

This risk of "end period dominance" calls for an investment policy that avoids major fluctuations in market value.[1] Pension plans, on the other hand, are virtually perpetual investment vehicles, funded to provide a stream of annuity payments to plan participants over a very long and highly predictable period; they can easily accept quite substantial market fluctuations during the long "interim" period.

That the investments of pension funds and profit sharing plans are not, in fact, differentiated on even such a powerful and basic

---

[1]Profit sharing plans can easily be designed to minimize this problem. In more and more companies, each plan participant has a separate account in which the asset mix can be adapted to the risk preferences of the individual and can be changed over time to reflect the worker's changing circumstances: all in growth stocks when young, shifting to a conservative balanced portfolio towards retirement, and so forth.

dimension as the stock-bond ratio, leads to the sobering conclusion that while investment policy conforming to the client's particular investment objectives may be honored in theory, it is little used in practice.

The differences in employees benefit plans can be substantial, but these differences will only matter if corporate executives vigorously represent the special characteristics of their company and their plan when basic investment policies are being formulated or reviewed.

It is hardly conceivable that senior corporate management would routinely delegate full operating responsibility for comparable millions of dollars[2] to regular operating divisional executives—let alone a manager not directly supervised by top management—with only such broad guidelines or instructions as: "Try to do better than average," or "You're the experts, see what you can do for us."

The real question is not whether portfolio managers are constructing portfolios to match the goals and objectives of each specific client. (The uninspiring reality is that they do not.) The relevant question is: Who is responsible for bringing about the requisite change? The pragmatic answer is that the responsibility is not going to be fulfilled by investment managers. It will be left to the client. Clients can and should accept this responsibility.

Clients can do more for their portfolio's long-term rates of return by developing and sustaining wise long-range policies that commit the portfolio to an appropriate structure of investments than can be done by the most skillful manipulation of the individual holdings within the portfolio.

In brief, clients should subordinate portfolio operations to investment policy, and should assert their responsibility for leadership in policy formation. This is not an investment problem that should be left to portfolio managers—no matter how skilled and conscientious they are—any more than, as Clemenceau observed, war should be left to the generals. It is the client's problem, and while responsibility for it can be abdicated, it really cannot be delegated.

---

[2]At some companies, pension fund assets are larger than the sponsoring corporation's net worth.

Only the client will know enough to speak with relevance and credibility to such important characteristics as the amount, timing, and certainty of flows *out* of the fund. Only the client knows his own or his organization's tolerance for changes in market prices—particularly at market extremes where it really matters—because it is at such stress periods when investment policies seem least certain and the pressure for change is most strong. For individual investors, only they will know their overall financial and investment situation—their earning power, their ability to save, their obligations for children's educational expenses, or how they feel about investments.

Corporate executives will know their pension plan's actuarial assumptions and how close to reality these assumptions really are; the company's tolerance for intrusions upon its quarter-to-quarter and year-to-year progression of reported earnings by a sudden need to fund a deficit in plan assets caused by an abrupt drop in market value of pension assets; the company's evolving philosophy of employee benefits and how benefit programs might be changed; the company's likeliness to increase benefits to retired plan participants to protect their purchasing power from the corrosion of inflation; and the tolerance of interim market fluctuations among staff, senior executives, and the board of directors. The "risk tolerance" of a corporate pension plan sponsor is not just the risk tolerance of the pension staff or even the senior financial officer: It is the risk tolerance of a majority of the board of directors at the moment of most severe market adversity.

Here are six important questions each client should think through, and then explain his own answers to the investment manager. (Investment managers would be wise to urge their clients to do this kind of "homework.")

First, what are the real risks of an adverse outcome, particularly in the short run? Unacceptable risks should never be taken. For example, it would not make sense to invest all of a high school senior's college tuition savings in the stock market because if the market went down, the student might not be able to pay the tuition bill. If the student's parents have been fortunate enough to win the "money game" so far, they can keep it that way simply by not continuing to play.

Second, what are the probable emotional reactions of clients to an adverse experience? As the axiom goes, some investors care about *eating* well and some care about *sleeping* well. The portfolio manager should know and stay well within the client's informed tolerance for interim fluctuations in portfolio value. The emphasis on *informed tolerance* is deliberate. Avoidance of market risk does have a real "opportunity cost," and the client should be fully informed of the opportunity cost of each level of market risk *not* taken.

Third, how knowledgeable about investments and markets are clients? Investing does not always make sense. Sometimes it seems almost perversely counterintuitive. Lack of knowledge tends to make investors too cautious during bear markets and too confident in bull markets—sometimes at considerable cost. Managers should be careful *not* to assume their clients will be more sophisticated than they really are.

Portfolio managers can help their clients by explaining the way capital markets behave—and misbehave—and clients can help educate themselves.

The client who is very well informed about the investment environment will know what to expect. This client will be able to take in stride those disruptive experiences that may cause other less informed investors to overreact to either unusually favorable or unusually adverse market experience.

Fourth, what other capital or income resources does the client have and how important is the particular portfolio to the client's *overall* financial position? For example, pension funds sponsored by large and prosperous corporations can reasonably accept greater market risk than can a college endowment, which may have difficulty raising capital to replenish losses. A retired widow usually cannot accept as much risk as can her alma mater.

Fifth, are any legal restrictions imposed on investment policy? Many endowment funds have restrictions that can be significant, particularly when they specify how income is to be defined or spent, or both.[3]

Sixth, are there any unanticipated consequences of interim fluctuations in portfolio value that might affect policy? A frequently cited example is the risk in a pension fund of being obliged to augment contributions if the portfolio's market value

---

[3]As William Carey and Craig Bright advocate in their fine study, *The Law and the Lore of Endowment,* restrictions should be carefully examined because they may not be as confining as they might initially appear.

drops below a "trigger" level built into the actuaries' calculations of current contributions.[4]

Each of these possible concerns should be rigorously examined to ascertain how much deviation from the normally optimal investment policy—broad diversification at a moderately above average market risk—is truly warranted. Understanding and using these insights into the specific realities of the particular client's situation and objectives is the basis upon which wise investment policies can be developed for each different portfolio.

In pursuing the goal of developing and using wise investment policies, we must recognize that most *institutional* funds such as pensions and endowments are *un*owned money: They do not really belong to anyone. There is no individual who can or would say "This is my money. *This* is what I want you to do with it. Or else." There are, in other words, no principals.

Second, we should recognize that those who are "at the controls" are usually only representatives of an organization and subject to after-the-fact criticism by powerful Monday-morning quarterbacks. These representatives have clear economic incentives to protect their careers: "It may not be my money, but it is my job."

Third, the careers of these institutional representatives seldom hinge on the work they do in setting investment policy or managing investment managers. Most have other more important functions, and almost all will hold their present reponsibilities for only a few years. They are *not* long-term players.

In such circumstances, what pattern of behavior would we expect of these representatives? Clearly they will be defensive in the "minimax," and will make their decisions with reference to a relatively short time period, say three to five years. They will not seek to optimize, they will seek the most acceptable near-term balance between desires for superior returns and avoidance of unusual or unorthodox positions. And above all, they will avoid any unnecessarily distressing risk to their own careers!

What are investment managers doing? The very same thing. They want to keep their accounts. They are understandably cau-

---

[4]Actuarial calculations have an apparent precision that Fellows of the Society of Actuaries would be among the first to caution are based on estimates and judgments.

tious. They are compromising with a defensive tilt, seeking "not to lose" over a three-to-five year horizon.

Observers of the paradox that haunts investment management say it is unrealistic to expect investment managers to risk strained client relationships by insisting on a well-conceived and carefully articulated investment policy with explicit objectives when their clients seem uninterested in going through the discipline.

For that, we must look not to the agents but to the principals. But in institutional investment management there *are* no principals. And if there often are no agents willing to act like principals, then we can be sure that the paradox will remain for a long time.

Escape from the paradox depends upon clients asserting their role as experts on their own needs and resources, and insisting on appropriate investment goals and policies.

6

Time

Time is Archimedes' lever in investing.

Archimedes is often quoted as saying, "Giving me a lever long enough, and I can move the earth." In investing, that lever is *time*.

The length of time investments will be held, the period of time over which investment results will be measured and judged, is the single most powerful factor in any investment program.

If time is *short*, the highest return investments—the ones an investor naturally most wants to own—will be undesirable, and the wise investor will avoid them. But if the time period for investing is abundantly *long*, the wise investor can commit without great anxiety to investments that appear in the short run to be very risky.

Given enough time, investments that might otherwise seem unattractive may become highly desirable. Time transforms investments from *least* attractive to *most* attractive—and vice versa—because, while the average expected rate of return is not at all affected by time, the range or distribution of *actual* returns around the expected average is very greatly affected by time. The longer the time period over which investments are held, the closer the actual returns in a *portfolio*[1] will come to the expected average.

---

[1] The actual returns on *individual* investments will, in contrast, be more and more widely dispersed as the time period lengthens.

As a result, time changes the ways in which different kinds of investments can best be used by different investors with different situations and objectives.

The conventional time period over which rates of return are calculated—their average *and* their distribution—is one year. While convenient and widely used, this particular 12-month time frame simply does not match the time available to all the different kinds of investors with all their different constraints and purposes. For example, some investors are investing for only a few days at a time while other investors will hold their investments for several decades. And it is the difference in time horizon that really matters.

To show how important time really is, let's exaggerate for effect, and look at the returns expected in a *one-day* investment in common stocks.

The typical stock's share price is $40, and the range of trading during the day might easily be from $39^1/_4$ to $40^1/_2$—a range of $1^1/_4$ or 3.1 percent of the average price for the day. Remembering that in today's market—with today's expectations for future inflation—the average annual rate of return for common stocks is approximately 15 percent, let's postulate that an investment in this hypothetical stock would have an expected daily return of 0.06 percent (15 percent annual return divided into 250 trading days) and a range around that expected average of plus or minus 1.55 percent (3.1 percent intraday range divided by two.)

Now, let's "annualize" that daily return of 0.06 percent and that 3.1 percent daily variation. The average annual expected rate of return would be 15 percent, but the *range* of returns around the 15 percent would be a daunting ± 387.5 percent! (In other words, the annual rate of return for a one-day investment in our hypothetical stock would be somewhere between a *profit* of 405.5 percent and a *loss* of 372.5 percent!)

Of course, no sensible investor would knowingly invest in common stocks only for a single day or month or even for a year. Such brief time periods are clearly too short for investments in common stocks, because the expectable *variation* in return is too large in comparison to the average expected return. The extra uncertainty incurred when investing in common stocks is not balanced by a sufficiently large or sufficiently sure reward. Such short-term holdings in common stocks are not investments: They are rank speculations.

On the other hand, this deliberate one-day burlesque of the conventional use of annual rates of return leads to a serious examination of the differences in investor satisfaction when the measurement period is changed. And this examination shows why an investor with a very *long* time horizon might well invest entirely in common stocks just as wisely as another investor with a very *short* time horizon would invest only in Treasury bills. The examination also shows why an intermediate-term investor would, as his time horizon extended outward, shift investment emphasis from money market instruments toward bonds and then toward more and more equities.

Both the constancy of the average *expected* rate of return— no matter what the time period—and the profound impact of time on the actual realized rate of return is clearly demonstrated in the charts in Figure 6–1.

The one-year-at-a-time rates of return on common stocks over the years are almost incoherent. They show both large and small gains and large and small losses occurring in what appears to be a random pattern. It seems absurd to "summarize" those wildly disparate one-year experiences as having any "average" rate ·of return.

Shifting to five-year periods brings a considerable increase in coherence or regularity. There are, for example, few periods with losses, and the periods with gains appear far more often and consistently. The reason is that as the measurement period lengthens, the average rate of return becomes more and more dominant vis-à-vis the single year differences.

Shifting once again to 10-year periods increases the consistency of returns significantly. Only one loss is experienced and most periods show average annual gains of 5 to 15 percent. Again, the power of the average rate of return—now compounded over a decade—overwhelms the single year differences.

Moving on to 20-year periods brings even more consistency to the experienced rate of return. There are no losses, only gains. And the gains cluster more and closely together around the long-term expected average rate of return.

Despite the obvious substantial differences in the range or distribution of returns in each time frame, there is one central constant: the *average* actual rate of return is almost the same in all cases. This is because the data shown are all samples from

FIGURE 6–1 Range of Returns on Common Stocks for Various Time Periods, 1950–80

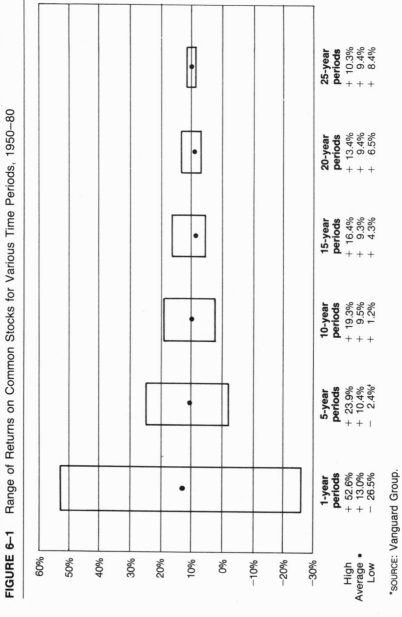

	1-year periods	5-year periods	10-year periods	15-year periods	20-year periods	25-year periods
High	+ 52.6%	+ 23.9%	+ 19.3%	+ 16.4%	+ 13.4%	+ 10.3%
Average ●	+ 13.0%	+ 10.4%	+ 9.5%	+ 9.3%	+ 9.4%	+ 9.4%
Low	− 26.5%	− 2.4%*	+ 1.2%	+ 4.3%	+ 6.5%	+ 8.4%

*SOURCE: Vanguard Group.

the same continuous stream of investment experience.

Appreciating that actual experiences in investing are samples drawn from a continuous stream of experience is vital to understanding the meaning contained in the data. Even in New England, the weather—when considered over a long period of time—becomes a sensible, reliable *climate* even though the days of bitter cold or sweltering heat seem individually so unpredictable, particularly as to the exact date of occurrance. Similarly, in investing, the patient observer can see the true underlying patterns that make the seemingly random year-by-year or month-by-month or day-by-day experiences not disconcerting or confusing, but rather splendidly predictable—on average and over time.

In weather and investments, larger and more numerous samples enable us to come closer and closer to understanding the normal experience from which the sample is drawn. It is this understanding of the normal experience that enables us to design our own behavior so we can take advantage of the dominant normal pattern over the long term, and not be thrown off by the confusing daily events that present themselves with such force.

The single most important dimension of investment policy is asset mix, particularly the ratio of fixed income investments to equity investments.

Discussions of asset mix have attracted considerable attention in recent years, particularly among pension managers. Their analyses shows that over and over again the trade-off between risk and reward is driven by one key factor: time.

Unfortunately, in most cases the time horizon being used is not chosen for the specific fund, but is instead a conventional five years. A five year "horizon" usually leads to the familiar 60:40 ratio of equities to debt. A 10-year horizon leads to an 80:20 ratio. A 15-year horizon typically results in a 90:10 ratio. And so it goes. The unfortunate reality is that none of these time horizons is "right" for a pension fund or a university endowment. They are all far too short for a fund with an investment horizon of 30 to 50 years or even more.

What is most disturbing about asset mix decisions is not that they are made with an inappropriately short time horizon, but that there is almost no evidence that such decisions are made deliberately and explicitly. For example, there is no evidence of differences in asset mix between such obviously different employee benefit plan as pension plans and profit sharing plans. Nor are there significant differences among pension plans with such obvious differentiations as companies with high actuarial rate-of-return assumptions versus companies with low actuarial rate-of-return assumptions; companies with an old work force versus companies with a young work force; companies with fast growth in earnings versus companies with little or no growth in earnings; or by the percent of fund obligations now funded or by the percent of corporate profits being paid into the plan as annual contributions.

The irony is that while their near-perpetual character enables pension funds to accept interim market risk better than any other type of investor, the typical pension fund was, in the late 1970s and early 1980s, only 50 percent in equities. In other words, the time horizon actually being used in managing the typical pension fund was not 30 years or 50 years, but only three or four.

These funds paid an opportunity cost in returns forgone. As it turned out, the cost of not being fully invested in stocks in 1982 and 1983 was very large. Investment history documents conclusively that the very first weeks of a market recovery produce a substantial proportion of the gains to be experienced. Yet, it is at the crucial market bottom that the market timer is most likely to be out of the market—missing "the best part."[2] But that is not the point at issue here. The point is that managers and clients should have taken such a cautious asset mix decision only after examining the inherent risks and rewards and deciding what policy would be best for them. Such powerful decisions should be made deliberately, and only after careful examination of long-term realities.

If more clients and managers insisted on such long-range policy reviews, their funds would typically be invested differently and would earn higher returns.

---

[2]Robert H. Jeffrey, "The Folly of Stock Market Timing," *Harvard Business Review*, July–August, 1984.

7

Returns

Investment returns come, as everyone knows, in two very different forms: quite predictable cash received from interest or dividends; and gains or losses in market price that are, particularly in the short run, quite *un*predictable. Investors devote most of their time and skill to trying to increase returns from changes in market prices—by outsmarting each other.

Changes in market price are caused by changes in the consensus of active investors of what the price of a stock ought to be. This consensus is determined by thousands and thousands of institutions and individuals constantly seeking opportunities for investment profit. To find these opportunities, investors study monetary and fiscal economics and political developments in all the major nations; visit hundreds and hundreds of companies; attend thousands of breakfast, lunch, and dinner meetings with corporate executives, economists, industry experts, securities analysts, and other experts; study reports and analyses produced in enormous volume by hundreds of companies and dozens of large brokerage firms; read extensively in the industry and trade press; and talk almost constantly on the telephone with people who have ideas, information, or insights with which these active investors might improve their investment performance.

In addition to studying the *rational* world, investors also study the irrational world of "investor psychology," public confidence, politics, and "market tone," because in the short run the markets—and market prices—are very human or nonrational. The ways in which investors perceive and interpret information and the ways they react to developments have great impact on market prices, particularly in the short run. So active investors are always looking for opportunities to capitalize on changes in other investors' opinions before changes in their own opinions are capitalized upon by other investors. Not all of the investors' interpretations and perceptions are "correct." Many, particularly in retrospect, seem very wrong.

Investment management in today's dynamic markets is a wonderful, turbulent, fascinating, hopeful, anguishing, stressful, and euphoric process of competing in the world's most free and competitive market against many talented and ambitious competitors for advantage gained from greater knowledge and wiser interpretation and better timing. (The irony is that for most investment managers and their clients most of this activity really does not matter—not because these investment managers are not talented, but because so many of their competitors are equally talented. It's not how good you are that counts, but how good you are compared with your competitors.)

For all the surface complexity in the process, two main areas are dominant in the evaluation of common stocks. The first is the general consensus of investors on the probable amount and timing of future earnings and dividends. The second is the consensus of investors on the discount rate at which this stream of estimated future dividends and earnings should be capitalized to establish its present value.

The consensus estimates of future dividends and earnings will vary among different investors and at different times due to changes in expectations for secular growth and cyclical fluctuations in unit demand; prices and taxes; discoveries and inventions; changes in the competition at home and abroad, and so forth. And over time, the discount rate considered appropriate will vary with many factors, among which the most important will be the perceived risk of the particular investment or investments of its general type and the expected rate of inflation.

The longer the future period over which estimates—both of earnings and dividends and of the discount rate—must be extended, the greater the day-to-day or month-to-month fluctuations in the stock price that will be caused by changes in the investors' consensus of present value.

As the time horizon over which an estimate extends is

lengthened, the impact of the estimated discount rate becomes more and more dominant (relative to estimates of future earnings and dividends) on the current market price of a security.

For investment value, on the other hand, as the holding period over which the investor owns an investment lengthens, the importance of the discount factor decreases and the importance of the dividends paid increases.

For the very long-term *investor*, the relative importance of earnings and dividends received is overwhelming. For the very short term *speculator*, everything depends upon the day-to-day and month-to-month changes in investor psychology (or in more formal terms, the appropriate discount rate) and what people are willing to pay. Like the weather, the average long-term experience in investing is never surprising, but the short-term experience is *always* surprising.

The history of returns on investment, as documented in study after study, shows three basic characteristics:

1. Common stocks have average returns higher than bonds, which in turn have higher returns than short-term money market instruments.
2. The daily, monthly, and yearly fluctuations in actual returns on common stocks exceed the fluctuations in returns on bonds, which in turn exceed the fluctuations on short-term money market instruments.
3. The magnitude of the period-to-period fluctuation in rate of return increases as the measurement period is shortened and decreases as the measurement period is lengthened. In other words, rates of return appear more normal over long periods of time.

The really impressive characteristic of investment returns is that the *variation* in year-to-year rates of return on common stocks dwarfs the average annual rate of return on stocks.

We now know that it is nonsense to say, "Common stocks have produced an average rate of return of 9 percent." This is an incomplete and misleading statement. Over the past 50 years, the actual returns have been between a *loss* of 43 percent, and a *gain* of 54 percent. While the geometric mean rate of return is about 9 percent, the standard deviation of actual returns around that mean is nearly 22 percent. And finally, we regret to say we cannot give you the sequence with which those returns will be experienced. They, of course, occur at random.

The two statements are remarkably different from one another—particularly for the investor who is suddenly and unexpectedly experiencing the most dreadfully negative year in what was so serenely described as the "normal" bell-shaped distribution. That's why investors and investment managers are learning to describe investment returns in statistical terms.

In addition to learning the importance of describing the distribution of returns around that mean, we have also learned to separate out the different components in the average rate of return and to analyze each component separately.

There are three main components in the average rate of return:

1. The risk-free rate of return.[1]
2. A premium over the risk-free to offset the expected erosion of purchasing power due to inflation.
3. A premium over the inflation-adjusted risk-free rate of return to compensate investors for accepting market risk.

Dividing total returns into these three classes of return makes it possible to compare the returns of each type of investment—stocks, bonds, and bills. This work has been done in a series of landmark studies by Roger Ibbotson and Rex Sinquefield, and the accompanying table from their book shows their major findings for the 55 year period 1926–81 (see Figure 7–1). The analysis is very informative.[2]

Treasury bills appear quite safe and reliable—in nominal terms, not adjusted for inflation—with positive returns in 54 to 55 years. However, when adjusted for inflation, returns are positive just less than 60 percent of the time: Even more impressive, the average annual rate of return on bills, after adjusting for inflation, is zero.

In other words, Treasury bills are usually no more than a haven from inflation. Most of the time, you do get your money back—with its purchasing power intact. But that is all you get. There is virtually no real return *on* your money, just the return *of* your money.

---

[1]There is no risk of default in a Treasury bill because if the government were short of money it would simply print more!

[2]Roger G. Ibbotson and Rex A. Sinquefield, *Stocks, Bonds, Bills, and Inflation: The Past and the Future*, Charlottesville, Va: Financial Analysts Research Foundation, 1982.

FIGURE 7-1   Wealth Indexes of Investments in the U.S. Capital Markets
1926–81

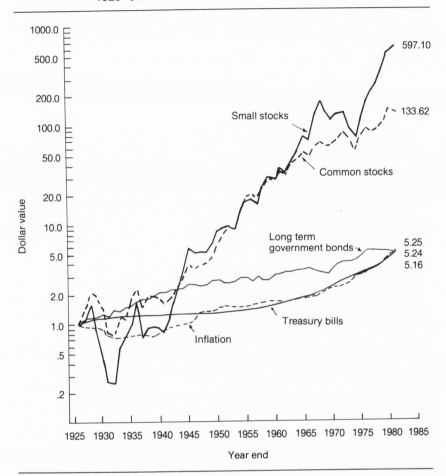

Long bonds produce higher returns, inflation adjusted, for
two reasons: corporate bonds involve a risk of default; and both
corporate and government bonds impose upon the investor an
exposure to market fluctuations due to their more distant maturity. Investors don't want such market price fluctuations unless they get a higher rate of return to compensate, so long
bonds pay a higher rate of interest—a maturity premium. The
maturity premium is estimated at 0.9 percent and the default
premium on high grade long term corporate bonds works out
at 0.5 percent. Adding these two premiums to the risk-free rate,
the inflation-adjusted annual real rate of return on long govern-

ment bonds is 1.0 percent and on long corporates, about 1.4 percent.

Similarly, the risk premium on common stocks is calculated at 6.1 percent, and the inflation-adjusted rate of return is, congruently, also 6.1 percent.

When the powerfully disruptive impact of inflation is removed, and when return experience is examined in reasonably long time periods, it becomes clear how consistent investment returns really are.

This consistency stems from two main factors:

a. Investors are sensibly consistent in requiring higher rates of return to compensate them for accepting higher market risk.

b. As the period over which returns are measured is lengthened, the short term volatility in returns caused by changes in the discount rate becomes less and less important and the expected dividend stream, which is more stable, becomes more and more important.

The central point is that we do not have and cannot hope to get perfectly precise or "correct" data on rates of return from investments in securities—any more than we can expect to get "correct" data by sampling any other complex, dynamic, continuous process, impacted by a multitude of large and small exogenous factors. However, we can get a very useful *approximation* of what returns have actually been and what they are most likely to be—and that is all we really need to establish basic investment policies for the long term.

Unless the investor buys in at the start of the period measured, sells out at the end, and takes his or her money out of the market, performance data are simply statistics. They describe samples from a continuous and very long-term process in which stock prices go through a "random walk" series of successive approximations of the actual present value of each stock based on continuously revised estimates of future earnings dividends and frequently changed capitalization rates (or discount rates).

Two further propositions on returns are important. First, the impact on returns of changes in the expected level of inflation can be enormous, particularly on common stocks which are virtually perpetuities. Such a change in the expected rate of inflation from approximately 2 percent in 1960 to approximately 10 percent in 1980 (along with other changes) caused a change in the required nominal average rate of return from common stocks from about 9 percent in 1960 to about 17 percent in 1980, and this produced a major reduction in stock prices. Inflation adjusted, the loss investors experienced during the adjustment was the worst in half a century.

A further increase in the expected rate of inflation would have further depressed stock prices. This would drop stock prices down to the level from which buyers would get sufficient returns—with the same future "real" earnings and dividends as previously expected—to offset the now expected rate of inflation, compensate for risk, and provide a risk-free real rate of return of "about 6 percent plus or minus 12 percent in two out of three years." A decrease in the expected rate of inflation would have the opposite effect, as we saw in 1982–85.

The second proposition on returns is that differences in rates of return that may appear moderate in the short run can, with compounding, multiply into very large and quite obvious differences in the long run. (When asked what he considered man's greatest discovery, Albert Einstein replied without hesitation: "Compound interest!")

The following table shows the compounding effect on $1.00 invested at different compound rates compounded over different periods of time (see Figure 7–2). It's well worth careful study— particularly to see how powerful is *time*. That's why time is the "Archimedes lever" of investment management.

FIGURE 7-2 Compound Interest over Time

Compound Rate of Return	Investment Period		
	5 Years	10 Years	20 Years
20%	$2.49	$6.19	$38.34
18	2.29	5.23	27.39
16	2.10	4.41	19.46
14	1.93	3.71	13.74
12	1.76	3.11	9.65
10	1.61	2.59	6.73
8	1.47	2.16	4.66
6	1.34	1.79	2.65
4	1.22	1.48	2.19

8

Risk

Risk is such a simple little word that it is amazing how many different meanings are given to it by different users.

Active investors typically think of risk in four different ways. One is price risk: You can lose money by buying stock at too high a price, and if you think a stock *might* be high, you know you are taking some price risk.

Another type of risk is called interest rate risk: If interest rates go up more than is now expected (and already discounted in the market), your stocks will go down. You'll know you were taking risk.

A third type of risk would be business risk. The company may blunder and earnings may not develop. If so, the stock will drop. Again you were taking risk.

In the extreme, the company may fail completely. That's what happened with Equity Funding, Penn Central, and Seattle First National Bank, and very nearly happened with Chrysler and International Harvester. As the old pros will tell you, "Now *that* is *risk!*"

They are right. But there is another way to look at risk that has come from the extensive academic research done over the past two decades; more and more investment managers and clients are using it, because there's nothing so powerful as a theory that works. Here's the concept:

Investors are exposed to three kinds of investment risk. One kind of risk simply *cannot be avoided*, but investors are rewarded for taking it. Two other kinds of risk *can be avoided* or even *eliminated,* and investors are not rewarded for accepting these unnecessary and avoidable kinds of risk.

Before exploring these three quite different kinds of risk more fully—and showing how investment managers and clients can use their understanding in establishing investment policy—let's pause to show the way active investors think about risk of the kind we'll soon see is *not* rewarded.

The basic assumption of all active investors is that they will do better than the market because they will discover and exploit opportunities for profit by buying stocks that are underpriced or by selling stocks or groups of stocks that are overpriced.

For active investors, the risk they take that their judgment will prove wrong is a cost they are willing to incur as they reach out for opportunity. They do not expect to be right all the time, but they certainly expect to have a good batting average. (As explained in Chapter 2, most will be disappointed.) What is important at this point in our discussion is that active investors should not expect to profit *because* they take risks on individual stocks or groups of stocks: They should expect to profit *in spite of* the risks taken (after compensating for their losses or errors.)

Now let's return to the theory that is so powerful and useful. As noted, investors are exposed to three kinds of investment risk. One kind of risk simply cannot be avoided, but it does pay investors for taking it. Two other kinds of risk can be virtually eliminated, and do not pay for being taken.

The risk that cannot be avoided is the risk inherent in the overall market. This market risk pervades all investments. It can be increased by selecting volatile securities or by using leverage, and it can be decreased by selecting securities with low volatility or by keeping part of a portfolio in cash equivalents. But it cannot be avoided or eliminated. It is always there. So it must be *managed.*

The two kinds of risk that can be avoided or eliminated are closely associated. One involves the risk linked to individual securities; the other involves the risk that is common to a group of securities. The first can be called individual stock risk, and the second can be called stock group risk.[1]

---

[1]Academic writers use slightly different terms to describe the same three types of risk: market risk is called systematic risk, individual stock risk is specific risk, and stock group risk is extra market risk. The terms used here

A few examples will clarify the meaning of stock group risk. Growth stocks will, as a group, move up and down in price in part because of changes in investor confidence and willingness to look more or less distantly into the future. (When investors are very confident, they will look far into the future when evaluating growth stocks.) Interest-sensitive issues such as utility and bank stocks will all be affected by changes in expected interest rates. Stocks in the same industry—autos, retailers, computers, and so forth—will share market price behavior driven by changing expectations for their industry as a whole. The number of common causes that affect groups of stocks is surely great, and most stocks belong simultaneously to several different groups. To avoid unnecessary complexity, and to avoid triviality, portfolio managers will usually focus their thinking on major forms of stock group risk.

The central fact about both stock group risk and individual stock risk is this: They *do not need to be accepted* by the investor. They can be eliminated. Unlike the risk of the overall market, risk that comes from investing in particular market segments or specific issues can be diversified away—to oblivion.

As a result, in an efficient market no incremental reward can or will be earned over the market rate of return simply by taking either more individual stock risk or more stock group risk. Either type of risk should be incurred only when doing so will enable the portfolio manager to make an investment that will achieve truly worthwhile increases in returns. The evidence is overwhelming that, while enticing, such ventures are not sufficiently rewarding.

The lack of reward for taking individual stock risk or stock group risk is important because the portfolio manager who takes such risks with his clients' funds can only hope to be rewarded by his superior skill—relative to the aggregate skill of all competing investment managers—in selecting individual stocks or groups of stocks that are inappropriately priced. As explained in Chapter 3, the investment manager who takes these risks can only profit if his competitors have made a mistake.

Clearly, such risks can be avoided by the simple and con-

---

seem clearer and more natural. Risk identified as either individual stock risk or stock group risk is the risk that the *price* of an individual stock or group of stocks will behave differently than the overall market—either favorably or unfavorably—over the time period for which investment returns are measured.

venient strategy of designing a portfolio that replicates the market: no deviations in portfolio composition, no deviations in rate of return relative to the overall market, and no stock group risk or individual stock risk.

Note that eliminating these two particular forms of risk does not mean all risk is gone. Overall market risk will always be there, and in the field of risk, that's the big one.

The great advantage of the "market fund," a portfolio that replicates the overall market, is this: Such a fund provides a convenient and inexpensive way to invest in equities, with the riskiness of particular market segments and specific issues diversified away.

Risk-averse investors are willing to accept lower rates of return if they can reduce the market risks they *must* take in investing. And they are willing to see other investors get higher rates of return as an inducement to accept a larger share of the unavoidable market risk. But they will not pay their risk-taking confreres to take risks that can quite easily be avoided altogether by "buying the market."

Market risk is different. Because it cannot be eliminated, risk-averse investors must and will accept a less-than-market rate of return in order to achieve a less-than-market risk. And by so doing, they proffer an above-average rate of return to investors willing to accept a greater-than-average market risk. This is why investors who accept more-than-average market risk—particularly over time—are rewarded with better-than-average market returns.

The level of market risk taken in an equity portfolio can be estimated with good accuracy by calculating the historical price behavior of the stocks in the portfolio (on a weighted average) relative to changes in the market as a whole.[2]

The optimal level of market risk—for the very long term investor—is moderately above the average. This level makes sense

---

[2]The market risk inherent in investing in any one market can, of course, be reduced in a multimarket portfolio by balancing investments in one market with investments in other markets that behave differently. This sort of diversification is an important motivation behind the interest in investing in real estate and in diversifying internationally. The stock markets of France, Hong Kong, Japan, Italy, and Australia fluctuate as much or more than the American market, but usually at different times and for somewhat different reasons. The multimarket portfolio with its investment in several different markets will have reduced the "unavoidable" market risk of any one market.

because many other investors are not free to take a very long term view; their investments will be liquidated sooner—for children's education or at the termination of a trust or for a host of other near-to-medium-term events for which plans must be made. Other investors are simply unable to look with calm forebearance on the abrupt and substantial day-to-day, month-to-month, and year-to-year changes in stock prices that will be experienced in an equity portfolio over the long term. These investors want less risk and less fluctuation—and are willing to pay a price to get what they want.

In summary, the total return to an equity investor has four components: (1) the risk free return; (2) an extra return to compensate for the riskiness or price uncertainty of investing in the overall equity market; (3) a potential extra return for investing in one or more particular groups of stocks or market segments that for various economic, business, or market psychology reasons might behave differently than the overall market; (4) a potential extra return for investing in specific stocks that, for the same sorts of reasons, might behave differently than the overall market.

In a similar manner, the risk accepted by the portfolio can be separated into the same kinds of component parts: risk associated with emphasis on specific stocks; risk associated with emphasis on or avoidance of particular groups of stocks or market segments that are influenced in similar ways by common causes; and risk associated with investing at all in equities.

Corresponding to each component of *return*—except the risk-free return—is a component of *risk*. Total risk consists of an overall equity market component plus a market segment risk plus a risk related to uncertainty about the price behavior of the stocks of individual companies relative to the overall market.

Market segment risk and specific issue risk can be diversified away, as explained above, but overall equity market risk cannot. Figure 8–1 shows vividly how the riskiness of a single stock consists primarily of specific issue risk and market segment risk, but that in a typical portfolio, these two kinds of risk are reduced to only a small part of the investor's total risk.

The chart also shows that the typical large pension fund with several different managers will have even more diversification and that this surfeit of diversification will further reduce the specific issue and market segment risks to a very small percentage of total risk.

FIGURE 8-1 How Diversification Reduces Nonmarket Risk

	Typical stock	Typical portfolio	Several managers	Many managers
▦ Specific issue risk	60%	4%	0.5%	0%
☐ Market segment risk	15	2	0.5	0
⧄ General market risk	25	94	99	100

This phenomenon of very great diversification so often experienced in large funds employing several managers—usually
with each manager chosen specifically because of his or her "different" style of investing, but with their differences tending to
cancel each other out—raises serious questions about very active
management in institutional investing versus passive management with above average market risk.

In investment management, we now know that the crucial
factor is not how to manage rates of return, but rather how to
manage market risk. By managing market risk, we mean doing
two things at the same time: (1) deciding deliberately what level
of market risk to establish as the portfolio's basic policy, and (2)
holding to that chosen level of market risk. Changes in the level

of market risk should only be made when there has been a deliberate change in basic, long term investment policy.

With market risk under control, the investment manager and his client can decide whether and when to accept any individual stock risks or stock group risks in order to capture extra profits. Note that while this part of investment management gets most of the attention by far from both managers and clients, it is is usually only a side show compared to the main force driven by the chosen level of market risk.

That managing market risk is the primary objective of investment management is a profound assertion. It is the core idea of this entire chapter. The rate of return obtained in an investment portfolio is a derivative of the level of market risk assumed—or avoided—in the portfolio; the consistency with which that risk level is maintained through market cycles; and the skill with which specific stock risk and stock group risk are eliminated or minimized through portfolio diversification, or are well rewarded when deliberately taken.

Recognition that risk drives returns instead of being simply a residual of the struggle for higher returns transforms the concept of investment policy.[3] We now know to focus not on rate of return, but on the informed management of risk.

---

[3] As a child, I assumed the pendulum in the grandfather's clock was driving the minute and hour hands *forward* rather than, as I later learned, holding the hands back and controlling the rate at which the weights could move them forward. For me, the concept of a clock will never be the same.

9

Building Portfolios

Whether investment management is primarily art or science has long been a favorite topic of informal discussion among professional investment managers, perhaps because the discussions are typically resolved quite cheerfully by demonstrating that since the practice of investment management is clearly not a science, it must therefore be an art.

Anyone who has observed gifted investors at work will recognize the art—subtle, intuitive, complex, and usually quite inexplicable—in selecting individual stocks or groups of stocks. The great artists are true heros of the profession—Phil Fisher, Ben Graham, John Neff, John Templeton, Ned Johnson, Dean LeBaron, Paul Cabot, Lord Keynes, Warren Buffett, and Rowe Price. These unusually talented investors—and others—add value to portfolios by seeing and seizing opportunities others miss or recognize only later. For these paragons, there is art in stock picking.

But for most investment managers, portfolio management is neither art nor science. It is instead a very special problem in engineering, of determining the most reliable and efficient way of reaching a specified goal, given a set of policy constraints, and working within a remarkably uncertain, probabilistic, always changing world of partial information and *mis*information, all filtered through the inexact prism of human interpretation.

While certainly far from perfect, recent advances in the

availability of data and the development of modern portfolio theory are providing investment managers—and their more sophisticated clients—with the tools and analytical frames of reference they need to understand and define the investment problem so it can be managed. (It would be a naive presumption to believe that the problems of managing an investment portfolio can be "solved." We must be willing to live with their being brought under reasonable control and being managed to a satisfactory standard of performance.)

As explained in Chapter 7, we now know that the real challenge in portfolio management is not how to increase *returns*— by buying low and selling high—but how to *manage risk* by deliberately taking appropriate risks that led predictably over time to increased returns.

The distinctive characteristic of effective portfolio management is the elimination of *unintended* risk associated with individual stocks or groups of stocks, and the deliberate assumption of intended market risk.

While it is possible to add value through brilliant stock picking, investments in individual stocks and bonds are best thought of as components to be used in building a well designed portfolio. They may be good components or poor components, but in the context of portfolio management, individual securities have value only to the extent they enable the investment manager to improve the portfolio as a whole by increasing the return or reducing risk or both. Portfolio management is investment engineering.

In line with the concept of portfolio management as a challenge in engineering, the portfolio design that eliminates avoidable and unintended risk and maximizes expected returns at a deliberately chosen level of market risk is an *efficient* portfolio. An efficient portfolio has greater expected return than any other feasible portfolio with equal risk, and less risk than any other feasible portfolio with equal expected return.

Once such an efficient portfolio has been constructed, it would not make sense to incur either individual stock risk or stock group risk unless such available risk were directly associated with—and judged worth taking in order to exploit—a specific opportunity to capture extra return.

The amount by which market risk and return can be magnified in a portfolio by investing in higher market risk—more volatile stocks—is not spectacular, but the benefits, over the very long run, can be worthwhile. A portfolio with a market risk that is 20 percent greater than the overall market average is feasible. A market risk much higher than that would be difficult to design into a portfolio and still have the portfolio well diversified. The number and variety of stocks needed to achieve good diversification and to provide that much market risk simply are not available in the market.

The expected "extra" rate of return for the portfolio with 20 percent more than average market risk would be, on average and over the very long term, 1.4 percent annually.[1] If 1.4 percent of incremental return over the market average return seems modest, remember that *no* sizable institutional investor has achieved that amount of annual incremental return over any sustained period of time!

Thus far, our discussion has concentrated on equity investments. Portfolio management for bonds is different in the details, but the main concepts are basically the same.

Like stocks, bonds present both individual bond risks and group risks. For example, bonds issued by companies in a particular industry will, as a group, change in value with major changes in that industry's economics. Bonds with particular call or refunding features in common will rise and fall as a group in relative market popularity. The normal difference in yield (and therefore price) between corporate and government bonds changes, causing larger or smaller spreads between corporates as a group and governments as a group.

It is important to note that bond rating agencies have found most of their rating errors caused by the difficulty inherent in estimating such group risks, not in estimating the individual risk of a particular issuer compared to other issuers in the same industry or group.

Bond portfolio management starts conceptually with a passive portfolio that represents the overall bond market. This baseline portfolio will be diversified across numerous issues to protect against the credit risk of individual issuers and will use a defensive, evenly spaced schedule of maturities to defend against adverse changes in interest rates. The overall quality of the portfolio and its average maturity will be set in concert with the client's risk preferences and potential liquidity needs.

As with equities, the historical evidence is that the risk of

---

[1]Calculated as follows: 120 percent × 7 percent return on equities over and above the 8 percent risk-free rate of return = 1.4 percent.

individual bonds can be substantially eliminated through diversification with the result that portfolios of medium-to-lower-grade issues do, after all actual losses through defaults on either interest or principal or both, provide higher net returns over time than higher-grade issues. Therefore, portfolio managers can increase risk-adjusted return by concentrating on medium-to-lower grade bonds.

Having established a well-diversified portfolio, the manager and client can then decide whether and how and when to deviate deliberately—if at all—from the "baseline" portfolio in efforts to increase returns by: buying or selling individual issues in anticipation of a recognition by other investors of a change in quality rating; switching from one sector of the market that is currently high in price relative to historical norms to another sector that is relatively low in price; selling an issue that is temporarily high in price (perhaps because of a market imperfection) and simultaneously buying an equivalent issue that is lower in price (the so-called arbitrage swap); or changing the average maturity of the entire portfolio—going for long maturities (and call protection) when interest rates are expected to fall, and shortening up on maturities when interest rates are expected to rise—both to an extent not already anticipated in the market's yield curve.

Even though most investment managers (and their clients) see their work as active, assertive, and offensive, the reality is and should be that portfolio management is primarily a *defensive* process.

In deliberate pursuit of wisely determined and explicitly stated objectives of the client, the purpose of the portfolio manager is to control risk and to limit or prevent surprises. The basic responsibility of portfolio managers, since the invention of insurance and pooled risk accounts in merchant shipping on sailing vessels hundreds of years ago, is to control and manage risk.

10

Why Policy Matters

The principal reason for articulating long-term investment policy explicitly and *in writing* is to enable the client and portfolio manager to protect the portfolio from ad hoc revisions of sound long-term policy, and to help them hold to long-term policy when short-term exigencies are most distressing and the policy is most in doubt.

History teaches that both investment managers and clients need help if they are to hold successfully to the discipline of long-term commitments. This means restraining themselves from reacting inappropriately to disconcerting short-term data and keeping themselves from taking those unwise actions that seem so "obvious" and urgent to optimists at market highs and to pessimists at market lows. The best shield for long-term policies against the outrageous attacks of acute short-term data and distress are knowledge and understanding committed to writing.

The misdemeanors of investment management are almost all due to an inadequate advance understanding by a client or portfolio manager (or both) of either the *internal* realm of client objectives or the *external* realm of capital markets and investments, or both. If a major decision is truly fiduciary in nature, it never needs to be done quickly. Time urgent decisions are *never* fiduciary.

All too often, investment policy is both vague and implicit, left to be "resolved" only in haste, when unusually distressing market conditions are putting the pressure on and when it is all too easy to make the wrong decision at the wrong time for the wrong reasons.

Such improvisational reviews typically result in a substantial shift from equities at temporarily depressed prices into bonds and other fixed income investments that will not rise in capital value with the next cycle of the equity market, and vice versa. Clearly, such ill-timed changes in asset mix—selling low and buying high—can be very harmful to the long-term returns of the portfolio.

Comparable harm is also done when recent returns have been higher than should be expected, and investment managers and their clients shed requisite caution and boldly increase the amount of market risk in the portfolio. This extra portfolio risk may soon magnify the impact of a subsequent market decline, exacerbate the normal investor anxieties, and lead to another of those ad hoc policy revisions that cause investors to "sell low" what they have previously "bought high."

Investors are people and, like all other people, make decisions based on their emotions when a cool, rational analysis would call for a very different action. Peter Bernstein puts the matter with disturbing succinctness: Investors like best those market movements that are most *adverse* to their long-term interests, and most *dislike* market movements that are, in fact, in their long-term interests. Here is why this curious proposition is so true.

Since investors will eventually profit most when they buy low, it is, clearly in the investor's long-term interest to have stocks *down* in price so he can buy more shares with each year's additional savings. With more shares purchased at lower prices, the investor will receive a larger stream of total future dividends for each additional investment than he would obtain with the same amount of money used to buy the same stocks at higher prices. In brief, rational investors should only want stocks to be low in price and should be pleased to see stocks going down— so they can buy more.

We should only want stock prices to be high when we are going to be *selling*—not just an attempt at market timing, but a final, permanent liquidation. Most long-term investors will be net buyers in future years, not sellers. They should want stocks to go down to nice low prices so they can buy more shares that will pay more dividends.

Yet, as much as we may be able to see that our long-term interests are best served by lower stock prices, who among us can honestly say we don't feel a warm glow of affection for stocks and markets that have gone up even though it means stocks are now more expensive to buy and future rates of return on our additional investments will be lower? But, we are wrong when we feel good about stocks having gone up and we are wrong when we feel bad about stocks having gone down.

This brings us back to the main reason for studying and understanding investments and markets: to protect our portfolios from ourselves. The problem, as Santayana so aptly put it, is that "those who do not study history are doomed to repeat it."

Psychologists studying anxiety and fear have found four characteristics make people more worried about the perceived riskiness of a situation than the realities would warrant: large scale consequences; beyond personal control or influence; unfamiliarity; and sudden occurrence.

As a result, we are more fearful of air travel (in which fewer than 30 people are killed and fewer than 350 hurt in a typical year) than of travel in cars (in which 30,000 people are killed yearly and 350,000 injured). We are more fearful of nuclear power accidents, which have caused zero loss of life, than of cigarette smoking, which causes 35,000 deaths every year. And we are disproportionately concerned about major drops in the stock market.

Most clients of professional investment managers experience great anxiety over large scale, sudden, and frightening losses in portfolio value primarily because they have not been well informed in advance that these events are expected by those who have studied and understand the long history of stock markets.

Such drops in the market are eminently predictable—not in their timing, but in their magnitude and suddenness. And it is in these periods of anxiety—when the market has been most severely negative and policies appear most acutely in doubt—that clients and managers predictably engage in ad hoc "reappraisals" of long-term investment policy.

The situation is understandable. Clients are not sufficiently informed about the true nature of investment markets and do get surprised. And investment managers are literally overwhelmed by information in written reports; private and group meetings with corporate executives, economists, and analysts; telephone calls; stock price quotations; and market transactions that give a compelling urgency to the here and now, and to what others are or may be thinking of doing.

The resulting excessive attention to the present and the immediate future not only produces the "group think" errors brilliantly explored by Gustave LeBon in his great book, *The Crowd*, but also distracts attention from careful study of the profound difference in the short run versus the long run nature of investments.

Investment managers and their clients can do a lot to improve long-term portfolio returns by being sure that both are well informed about the realities of the investment environment in which the portfolio will be managed. Clients should ask their managers to review for them the rates of return and patterns of deviation away from the averages over the past decade or longer, explaining as carefully as possible why the markets moved as they did. Thoughtful, objective study of the past is the best (and also the least costly!) way to develop an understanding of the basic nature of investments and markets. Markets always have been and always will be surprising, but there is no justification for managers or clients being amazed or shaken by any market development.

Only with shared understanding of the nature of investing and capital markets will investment managers and their clients escape the present paradox in which little or no attention is devoted to the truly important work of developing and adhering to wise and appropriate investment policies that can, over time, achieve realistic and relevant investment objectives.

11

The Purpose of Policy

The high purpose of investment policy, and of the systematic discovery process prerequisite to it, is to establish useful guidelines for investment managers that are genuinely appropriate to the realities both of the client's objectives and the realities of the investments and markets. These are the internal and the external realms of investing, and investment policy must be designed to work well in both realms. In addition, good investment policies are "right" for both the long term and for the many short term periods that will be experienced in the market.

The value of a set of investment policies depends upon the understanding incorporated in them. First come the client's objectives and tolerances of risk. This is the responsibility of the client to develop and of the manager to understand. Second is the external realm of investments and markets, which is the investment manager's responsibility to understand and explain fully to the client.

Developing understanding of both dimensions of investment policy and how they can be fit together is a puzzle well worth working out. Investment policy is the explicit linkage between the client's long-term investment objectives and the daily work of the investment manager. If policy is *not* determined through carefully developed mutual understanding, it *will* be determined in uninformed, anecdotal "ad hocracy." To the extent that both client and investment manager understand the realities of the

situation as a whole, they will be able to understand what individual bits of data and specific events mean and do not mean
for the portfolio they are managing together.

The usefulness of investment policy depends on the clarity
and rigor with which investment objectives and the policy
guidelines established to achieve those objectives are stated.

The new investment language derived from modern portfolio
theory makes it relatively easy to specify investment objectives
and policies, and to measure portfolio operations to be sure they
are in conformance with agreed-upon policy. This language makes
genuine investment counseling possible, and should make it feasible for each portfolio manager to achieve excellent performance—not by heroically beating the market, but by faithfully
and sensibly carrying out realistic investment policies to achieve
agreed upon objectives for each client.

It is now practical for investment managers and clients to
agree objectively on each of these important policy dimensions:

1. The level of market risk to be taken.
2. Whether the level of risk is to be sustained or varied as
   markets change.
3. Whether individual stock risk or group risk are to be taken
   or avoided, and the incremental rate of return which such
   risks, when taken, are expected to produce in the portfolio.

Where deliberate differentiation from the market is expected
of the investment manager, it will always be wise to establish
explicit agreement as to the nature of the differentiating investments that could be made, the circumstances under which
they may be made, and the investment concept that gives the
manager and client confidence that they will achieve favorable
incremental results by taking action.

The conceptual simplicity of setting an explicit policy on
market risk and agreeing on how the portfolio will be differentiated from a fully diversified market fund is clearly appealing
in theory. As might be expected, there are practical problems
with the implementation. Because investing is a sampling process, the measurement of performance, as we will see in more
detail in Chapter 12, can only be done in probabilistic terms.
In measuring investment portfolios, we now have good tools,
but we do not have precision instruments. There are difficulties
with so-called sampling errors, because companies change and

stocks change in their investment characteristics. Even if we strive to estimate and adjust for these changes, there will be "noise" in the data that investment managers and their clients are working with. We have a new technology that enables us to communicate more efficiently than before; but the technology is still imperfect, and communication will require patience and tolerance.

There are two major reasons for producing good investment policy guidelines. First in the minds of many is to have a standard by which to monitor managers. As important as this is, the other reason is paramount: to decide what each client's own realistic long-term investment goals should be.

Time, as we have seen, is the single most important factor that separates the appropriate investment objective of one portfolio from the appropriate objective of another portfolio. Specifically, it is the length of time over which the portfolio can and will remain committed to a sustained investment policy, and over which the client will patiently evaluate investment results versus his objectives and policies.

Liquidity should not be given separate consideration in a well diversified portfolio *provided* that portfolio is invested in the kind of securities appropriate to its portfolio duration. For example, even the largest equity portfolio could easily and efficiently be liquidated in a year.

But if only a year's time were available to the portfolio, it should not be invested in equities at all. It should be in money market instruments for safety of principal protection against unanticipatable changes in market price. Sufficient liquidity always comes along automatically when investment policy is soundly conceived and implemented.

A puzzling practice, commonly followed in managing pension funds, is maintaining so-called liquidity reserves. The basic reality of the typical pension fund is that it will have a positive cash flow from contributions every year for another generation or more, and so has no need whatever for a liquidity reserve.

Income requirements are excluded from this discussion of investment policy because the rate of return for an investment portfolio cannot be increased just because a client wants more money to spend. It is indeed a curious idea that the investment objective for a portfolio should be set according to the funds the investor wants to spend each year. Sometimes this idea shows up in pension funds where the actuarial rate of return assumption will be put forth as a guide to investments. Sometimes it shows up with college presidents insisting on higher endowment fund income to make up for operating deficits. And sometimes it arises when personal trust funds are asked to finance a more expensive way of life. In all its forms, this practice is nonsense. On the contrary, instead of spending decisions influencing investment decisions, it should be the other way around. Spending decisions should most definitely be governed by the investment results—which follow from investment policies.

Investment policy should be separated from investment operations because they are such different responsibilities. Typically, however, responsibility for both investment policy and operating management of the portfolio are "delegated" to investment managers. Mixing together investment policy and portfolio operations—problem definition and problem solving—and delegating *both* to investment managers is not appropriate.

Formulation of long-term investment policy should be clearly and explicitly separated from the operating responsibilities of portfolio management. Only by separating portfolio operations from policy formation can responsibility and accountability be established for each of these two different aspects of investment management.

Portfolio operations should clearly be the responsibility of the investment manager. Policy is the responsibility of the client. Of course, they are not kept in isolation from each other. Operating performance will be evaluated objectively against the specified policy intention to be sure operations are in accord with policy. And investment policy will be evaluated objectively against long-term returns in the portfolio to be sure the policies are realistic.

An important advantage arising from the separation of investment policy from portfolio operations is the opportunity to control portfolio managers who, because they are human, are tempted to move away from long-term policy—particularly at the high and low points in a market cycle—too cautiously minimizing market risk at lows and too boldly accepting greater risk at the high point.

Segregating responsibility for investment policy from responsibility for portfolio operation is an essential first step in the work of managing the managers—removing the "what" and obliging them to concentrate entirely on the "how"—so their natural preoccupation with present market conditions will not corrupt the portfolio's long term policy. The time horizons of investment managers are typically shorter, often much shorter, than the client's time horizon. Clients should understand this and insist on having *their* time horizons prevail.

Having established investment objectives that are realistic in the market context and appropriate to the time horizon and risk preferences of the investor, it is appropriate to specify the investment policies to be followed by the investment manager in pursuit of these stated objectives.

It is by direct comparison with these explicit investment policies—and *only* by comparison with these explicit policies—that the operational performance of the investment manager should be measured and evaluated.

For example, it would be both unfair and misinforming to attempt an evaluation of the operational performance of a portfolio of growth stocks (or utility stocks or foreign stocks or high yield stocks) by comparing its results with the overall market averages, because such a comparison is evaluating a mixture of both policy *and* operations that should be examined separately. Specifically, the operational performance of a growth stock portfolio should be critiqued in comparison with an index of growth stocks or portfolios of growth stocks. In the same way, a manager of utility stocks should be evaluated only and always by comparison with the investment opportunities available in utility stocks, just as the manager of a portfolio of Japanese stocks should be evaluated only in comparison with the Japanese market and not in comparision with the British, Hong Kong, or American markets.

On the other hand, the *policy* of investing in growth stocks (or utility stocks or Japanese stocks) would be critiqued by examining the superior of portfolios of growth stocks (or utility stocks, or Japanese stocks) in comparison with other alternative types of stocks and to the market as a whole, over relatively long periods of time.

All too often, a portfolio manager has been praised or blamed for the favorable or adverse impact of policy over which she or he had no control. And in some cases, the portfolio manager has been credited with "good" performance when, in fact, poor operational performance hindered the attainment of even higher returns that would have resulted from more carefully following an effective policy.

Just as operating performance can be evaluated against policy, policy can be evaluated against performance. If the portfolio manager does not achieve the intended investment result, should the manager be kept and the policy changed? Perhaps the objective is too high. Perhaps the policy is too restrictive for the objective sought. The point is that we can learn from experience if we reflect thoughtfully on what our experience really means.

From time to time, perhaps once every two or three years, a systematic and comprehensive examination of the client's needs and objectives, market experience, and investment policy would be appropriate. While a review of actual results could be moderately useful in critiquing policy, most of the information relevant to a basic examination of investment policy will come not from the specific portfolio, but from more complete—and more relevant—analyses of major sectors of the investment market over very long periods of time.

If the policy is found inappropriate, it should be changed and the new policy made explicit to the portfolio manager. If the operating performance of the portfolio manager does not conform with policy, the manager should be replaced even if such deviation from stated policy resulted in a higher rate of return than would have been earned by following stated policy. (Of course, an incompetent portfolio manager would also be replaced, but this is a far easier decision to make.)

A few simple tests of investment policy are these:

1. Is the policy carefully designed to meet the real needs and objectives of this specific client?
2. Is the policy written so clearly and explicitly that a *competent stranger* could manage the portfolio and conform to the client's intentions?
3. Would the client have been able to sustain commitment to the policies during the capital markets that have actually been experienced over the past 50 or 60 years— particularly over the past 10 years?
4. Would the investment manager have been able to maintain fidelity to the policy over the same periods?
5. Would the policy, if implemented, have achieved the client's objectives?

Sound investment policies will meet *all* of these tests. Do yours?

12

Performance Measurement

Performance measurement is least useful when needed most—and is needed least when it could be most effective.[1] This chapter explains why.

As the investment manager is given more and more discretion to deviate from a market fund and to take more and more risks of different kinds—market risk, group risk, and individual stock risk—the difficulty of determining how much of any specific period's portfolio return is due to skill or chance increases rapidly.

Performance data that are sufficiently timely to have relevance for practical decisions on how well a manager is really doing, and whether a manager should be changed, may be based on too small a sample or too short a time period to provide information with enough accuracy for decisions. And results for longer time periods—which offer greater accuracy—will not be sufficiently timely to be relevant for current decisions on how well managers are doing, unless the results are overwhelmingly good or bad.

Measurements of a portfolio investment performance do not, at least in the short run, "mean what they say." Performance

---

[1]Professor Barr Rosenberg estimates it would require 70 years of observations to show conclusively that even 200 basis points of incremental annual return resulted of superior investment management *skill* rather than chance.

measurement services do not report "results." They report statistics. These statistics describe samples drawn period by period from a most unusual and continuous process—the process of managing complex, changing portfolios of securities in the context of a large, dynamic, always changing, and often turbulent free and competitive capital market. The stocks and bonds in the portfolios are frequently changed; companies and their businesses are always changing in many different ways; and the factors that most affect the prices of securities (fear, greed, inflation, politics, economic news, business profits, investors' expectations, and so forth) never cease to change.

So long as the portfolio is not being cashed in, this multi-dimensional set of change forces will go on and on revising the value of the portfolio. There are no real "results" until the process stops, and the portfolio is finally liquidated.

Since each investment manager's actual performance will—like the market's return—be drawn from a bell shaped probability distribution around a mean or average annual rate of return, investment objectives and performance measurements should be understood and specified in terms of both the mean or average rate of return and a distribution around that mean.

Recognizing that measurements of performance are statistics leads to an appreciation that, as with any series of statistics, each data point must be read not as an exact number but only as an *approximation* of an exact number.

For users of performance measurement, the big problem is separating three very different factors that are mixed into the overall performance data. One factor is the "sampling error" or the probability that the statistics do not precisely equal the facts. As in any sample, there will be imprecision or uncertainty. In investment performance data, the sampling error is the degree to which the particular portfolio, for the particular time period, is a good or a biased sample of the manager's work.

The second factor is that during the measurement period, the market conditions may have been a favorable or unfavorable environment for the particular manager's way of investing. For example, managers of small-capitalization stocks have had a very favorable market environment during the past decade. As a result, they have all "looked better than they really were." This is why most investment managers want to be measured over at least one full market cycle.

The third factor is the skill—or *lack* of skill—of the investment manager. This is what many clients and managers most want to measure. But here's the rub: In the very short run, sampling errors will have a much larger impact on the measured results than will the manager's skill.

To be specific, it would not be at all unusual for an investment manager's results to be in a range that was plus or minus 2 percent of the return that would be expected most of the time from a broadly diversified portfolio with the same level of market risk. As noted earlier, it would take many years of performance measurement to know whether the *apparently* superior results were due to the manager's skill or just to good luck.

A major problem for the investment managers and for their clients is the considerable dispersion in performance being produced by the same investment managers when managing portfolios with the same investment policies. Results should be the same, but the differences are substantial. For the investment manager, such dispersion is clearly an important problem in quality control.

For clients, a key problem will be in deciding how to interpret the results. Should a disappointed client accept the manager's assurances that below average results will surely be reversed in the coming period and that the client should stay? Or should the client reject the assurance, assert that the manager is "out of control," and terminate the relationship?

One thing is certain: Clients should insist on full disclosure of the performance of *all* the manager's portfolios so they can get a good sample of the manager's overall achievement. Clients should not try to infer the manager's overall performance from their own portfolio—a sample of one!

Information is data with a purpose. Because performance measurement can only be useful when a valid standard has been clearly established, performance measurement depends on a clear and explicit investment policy. And the purpose of regular measurements of portfolio performance must be to determine whether current portfolio *operations* are in faithful accord with long-term *policy*.

Performance measurement cannot and will not be useful in measuring results. Only an approximate answer can be given to a question like "What rate of return was earned in this quarter?" and that approximation will not be useful unless results are extreme. However, quite useful information can be drawn from performance measurement on the investment *process*. If portfolio operations have not been in accord with agreed policy and the investment manager's agreed upon mission, it is not really important whether current portfolio results happen to be above (lucky client) or below (unlucky client) the results that would be expected had policy been followed faithfully. In either case, the truly important information is that the portfolio and the portfolio manager are out of control. Sooner or later, this lack of control will show up in losses—uncontrolled and unrecoverable losses.

The impossibility of using short or even intermediate term performance measurement to manage managers by acting on "results" is what makes it so essential that clients and investment managers establish and sustain wise long-term investment policies.

There are other practical problems with performance measurement, particularly when used to measure whether a portfolio is or is not "within policy."

First, estimates of the risk of individual stocks and the risks of groups of stocks are probabilistic estimates of *future* price behavior based on the best available estimates of *past* behavior. While past patterns are usually our best available guide to likely future patterns, the future is sure to differ in significant measure from the past.

Second, the relationship between the "market" and a specific stock or portfolio of stocks is not constant. The relationship drifts. Consequently, the past will not be a perfectly reliable basis upon which to estimate the current or the future behavior of a stock or group of stocks.

Third, the amount of "drift" in the relationship over time will be less for stocks of major companies in established industries, and will be more for stocks in small or marginally successful companies, particularly in rapidly changing industries.

Fourth, even the most rigorous statistical description of individual stocks or groups of stocks are themselves estimates and are stated in terms of statistical probabilities, with the implicit understanding that there will be a distribution of actual experience around the expected mean.

Fifth, just one or two decisions—perhaps brilliantly skillful, perhaps lucky, perhaps both—can make a powerful difference to the reported performance of a portfolio. The classic example was the impact of a spectacularly successful, but almost accidentally made, investment in Digital Equipment. With it, American Research and Development (AR&D, a venture capital fund) significantly outperformed the market averages. Without it, AR&D would have underperformed the market during its 20 year life. Professional investment managers will recognize how often one of their portfolios has enjoyed far better results than another portfolio simply because, when implementing a strategic decision to invest heavily in an industry group, the stock used in one portfolio did very well while the stock used in another portfolio did badly.

Sixth and most important is the problem of "end period dominance." Almost always, the most important factor in the reported performance of an investment manager is not his or her skill, but is the choice of starting date and ending date. Many of the most impressive "gee whiz" charts of investment performance become quite ordinary by simply adding or subtracting one year at the start or the end of the period shown.

More and more clients and investment managers are quite properly dissatisfied with the convention of comparing the results of their portfolio to the results of a group of other portfolios of similar size which do not necessarily have the same long-term investment policies. A portfolio's operations should only be judged in comparison with its policy commitment and the results that should reasonably be expected given that policy.

At the very least, results for one portfolio should be compared only to funds with a similar prescribed level of market risk. And one of the key criteria on which performance should be measured is this: Did the portfolio manager keep the portfolio's market risk at the level specified in the statement of investment policy?

In addition, it would be more equitable and more informative to compare a portfolio's results with other portfolios with a similar mission: growth stock portfolios versus growth stock portfolios; conservative stock portfolios versus conservative stock portfolios; "small cap" stock portfolios to "small cap" stock portfolios, and so on.

In the same vein, the performance of an equity portfolio should be based on the total assets available for equity investment, not just the portion that happened to be in stocks—with cash positions excluded. The same applies to bond portfolios: Cash reserves should be counted in, not counted out. (Whether the use of cash reserves helped or hurt performance compared with a fully invested portfolio can and should be examined separately.)

For balanced accounts, the equity portfolio (cash reserves included) should be measured in comparison to similar equity funds and the bond portfolio (cash reserves included) should be compared to similar bond funds, and the impact of shifts in the stock/ bond mix should be reported and examined separately to see if these shifts in asset mix are contributing to overall results.

One of the great frustrations thoughtful investment managers have had with typical performance measurement is that bad decisions with favorable outcomes are often well received by innocent clients while good decisions with temporarily unfavorable outcomes can lead to the loss of an account. (This problem has been particularly common in recent years for investment managers specializing in growth stocks.)

More serious—because it is more common—is the pattern of clients choosing managers just after they have had "their kind of market," and imputing to these managers a special set of skills and genius that will be impossible to sustain after that market environment changes.

The final problem with performance measurement is its perverse tendency to stimulate counterproductive thinking and behavior by directing both the portfolio manager's and the client's interest and attention to the short-term operating results and away from long-term policy. The process of measuring will almost certainly influence the phenomenon being measured, as the physicist Heisenberg elucidated years ago with his "Principle of Interdeterminacy." There is a strong human tendency to think about the phenomenon being measured in the time interval used in the measuring, and to let the measurement interval dominate the time horizon actually used. Short-term thinking is the enemy of long-term investment success.

Since what is measured—and rewarded or penalized—and how often and by what standard will surely influence and may even become a dominant determinant in what investment managers will seek to achieve, clients must be sure they and their managers are measuring the right things the right way over the most relevant time period.

A form of Gresham's law can easily develop with both investment managers and corporate executives allowing concern with short-term operating results to drive out thoughtful concern with the longer-term policy concerns. (Quarterly performance, as we've just discussed, really can't be "measured." The sample is too small to give useful information.) This can easily lead to short-term operating results dominating long-term policy, with portfolio risk levels being reduced after adverse results and risk levels being increased after recent favorable operating results. Both are clearly counterproductive.

If the risk level is to be changed, it would make more sense to change it in the opposite direction, reducing risk after recently favorable results, and increasing risk after recently adverse results. Taking this counterintuitive action is, of course, very difficult to do—for both managers and for clients.

The main reason for measuring performance is to improve client-manager communication. The purpose of performance measurement is not to provide answers, but rather is to identify questions that clients and managers should explore together to be sure they have a good mutual understanding of what is contributing to and what is detracting from investment performance.

Central to good client-manager communication is information that shows whether the portfolio is being managed in accordance with agreed upon policy, particularly policy on market risk and on the type of security in which the manager is expected to specialize. The impact of these two policy parameters should be measured and reported on a regular basis.

The final area of "performance measurement" is clearly qualitative. Does the manager's explanation of his or her decisions make good sense? Is the manager doing as promised—making the kind of decisions that were "advertised"? Are the manager's actions consistent with his or her words at the previous meeting? When the manager changes the portfolio's structure, do the explanations make good common sense? As a thoughtful, interested client, do you find your confidence in the manager's abilities, knowledge, and judgment rising as you have more and more discussions—or is it falling?

Clients should give real weight to these "soft" qualitative factors because over and over again, this is where the best signals of real trouble first surface—long before the problem is evident in the "hard" qualitative data.

Even more important, wise clients have been able to stay with managers that made good qualitative sense even when the quantitative measures of performance were disappointing because the manager happened to be temporarily out of tune with the market. In many cases, subsequent performance has been very rewarding to both manager and client.

13

Managing Managers

Very few investment managers and very few clients are well satisfied with their present relationships. And it's their own fault. Too little attention is devoted by either clients or managers to designing and developing truly successful relationships. While investment managers can readily be faulted for not taking more initiative in this area, the primary responsibility does and always will rest with the clients.

Great clients make great firms, and clients of investment managers can do real service for their managers by combining three attributes: rigorous insistence on adherence to the explicitly agreed-upon mission; candor in discussing areas of dissatisfaction or uncertainty; and patience with the understandably emotional nature of investment managers—encouraging the glum and disappointed, cautioning the euphoric and self-assured.

Clients should assert themselves in developing good working relationships with investment managers for several reasons. First, as discussed in Chapter 4, clients know (or certainly ought to know) what is unusual and important about their organization's investment objectives. And it is the client's responsibility to project this knowledge into the process of formulating long-term objectives and investment policy.

Second, investment managers are so deeply immersed in the demanding details of daily investment operations that it is implausible that they would—alone and unaided—find time and interest to think through the specific circumstances of each client and develop sensitively separate policies for each.

Third, the real need in most investment relationships is not for more *investment* management, but for more *management* management, and this set of skills is far more likely to be found among corporate executives, foundation trustees, and makers of trusts with general management experience and orientation than among investment management specialists.

Finally, it is the client who has the most to gain from developing successful and purposeful relationships. While the manager can lose the account, his downside risk is the loss of a fee; the client's downside risk is no less than the health of his whole portfolio.

Here are some suggestions on how to be a good client. First, start by knowing yourself and your organization and what your investment objectives and staying power really are. Your capacity to tolerate investment adversity needs examination in different time frames. For example, it's one thing to know your ability to handle what might be called quarter-to-quarter fluctuations. They are relatively modest and soon reversed. It's another to absorb and accept a full bear market, particularly one that lasts longer and plummets more than normal.

The perspective within which to test yourself is not from the calm armchair of the market historian who can see "how it all worked out." Instead, you'll want to think very carefully about the way you would feel and might react to the dreadful experience of a severe bear market at its worst moment, when the next stage is not known and may be even worse! This kind of candid self-critique will help you determine your true investment staying power.

Determining your tolerance for pain and your investment staying power will provide you with the basis upon which you can set the level of market risk that you can and will live with. Don't overcommit. Know your internal realities, and stay within your own limitations. As my father, Raymond W. Ellis advised: "Never risk more than you know you can afford to lose."

Second, learn to understand the *external* realities of the investment markets and do not expect more of your managers than they will be able to deliver. If you insist on "beat the market" performance, you *will* find managers who will make the promise. But can they keep it?

Third, select managers who are clearly competent to complete the mission you have in mind for them, who understand the mission and accept it, and with whom you would genuinely enjoy working.

Finally, strive always to discipline yourself to keep faith with your own commitment to a steady, long-term program. Try to follow the advice of Caesar: *De minimus non curat praetor!* (Don't be concerned with small matters!)

The main features of mutually advantageous manager-client relationships are not difficult to describe. First, the relationship should be designed and intended to last a long time. Changing managers is costly and disruptive for both manager and client, and usually comes only after an unhappy series of misunderstandings and mistakes leads to endemic mistrust.

As in any good business relationship, the responsibilities and undertakings of each party should be both realistic and clear. In particular, the investment manager's "mission" should be both explicit and in writing, and mutually agreed upon. It should be within the competence of the investment manager; it should be realistic and reasonable relative to the market; and it should be sufficient to satisfy the client's legitimate and informed expectations. If these three criteria are *not* being met, the client should get together with the investment manager until they have agreed on a mission statement that does meet all three tests.

Second, the relationship will usually be centered upon quarterly or semiannual meetings, organized to achieve the success in working together desired by both investment manager and client. Before each meeting, an agenda should be prepared by the client and all relevant documentation should be provided, usually by the manager, with ample time for careful preparation by both manager and client. (The emphasis on *relevant* documentation is deliberate: It takes little genius to flood a meeting with sufficient trivia to camouflage the central issues.)

Each meeting should begin with a careful review of the investment manager's mission—the agreed upon investment policies of the portfolio through which the manager is expected to accomplish the mutually intended long-term objective—to see if any modification in either objective or policy is appropriate. If they have no changes in mission to propose, both client and investment manager should explicitly reaffirm the mission statement. If either client or manager wishes to propose a change, the proposal and the rationale supporting it should be prepared in advance and distributed as one of the meeting preparation documents so all participants can study and think through the proposed change. There should, of course, be no surprises in this most important part of the meeting.

Discussion of specific portfolio operations—purchases and sales of specific securities—should be on an exception basis and should be brief. This portion of the meeting should *not* be "interesting." Clients should not accept colorful recitations of war stories or capsule reviews of specific stocks: They are fun, but they are only entertainment. Instead, this part of the meeting should be a straightforward confirmation that the manager has sensibly and faithfully followed agreed-upon policy. Like a successful medical examination, the review of operations should be thorough, expeditious, and conclude with the assurance, "as expected, everything is fine."

At most, the review of operations and reaffirmation of the investment manager's mission should take half an hour. The balance of the meeting time, usually another half hour, can best be devoted to a thoughtful and detailed discussion of almost any one topic of importance to both the client and the manager.

At least once each year, the topic should be a candid review—led by the client—of the client's overall financial situation and the context into which the investment portfolio fits.

Similarly, it will usually be relevant for the investment manager to devote one meeting to a discussion of his organization's professional and business development—with particular emphasis on the investment management firm's long-term business and professional policies and commitments—and the importance to his firm of the kind of account represented by the client.

Other meetings can constructively be devoted to discussions of a major economic development, a major portfolio commitment, or discussion of the changing economics or investment attraction of a particular industry. The important purpose of these topical discussions is to enable the client to take a deep look into the thinking process of the investment managers.

Meetings should *not* be used as they usually are for a brief Cook's tour of the investment world that might include superficial comments on the economic outlook, recent changes in interest rates, a review of minor changes in the weightings of industry groups in the equity portfolio, a quick recap of modest shifts in quality ratings in the bond portfolio, and concluding with some interesting insights into specific decisions.

Such discussions can easily deteriorate into a superficial "show and tell" report of current events. Without really digging into any of the major decisions made, they can use up the time that might otherwise be devoted to serious discussions of subjects of potentially enduring importance to a successful relationship— and to the portfolio.

A written summary (of perhaps three to five pages) should be prepared and distributed after each meeting and kept for future reference. One good suggestion would be to have alternating meetings summarized by the clients and investment managers.

Meetings should not be used to bring new members of the client's investment committee up-to-date. Such catch-up briefings should be conducted separately, perhaps earlier on the same day as the main meeting. With a good written record of each prior meeting, these catch-up briefings can be accomplished both quickly and reliably—to everyone's benefit.

The most important contribution clients can make to a successful relationship with an investment manager is to select the right manager to begin with. Of course, the first step in selecting the right manager is to know what investment mission the chosen manager will be expected to fulfill.

Prospective investment managers should be examined in three major areas: professional investment competence; commitment to client service; and soundness of business strategy. Of the three areas, professional investment competence is quite properly given the greatest attention.

A prospective investment management firm should have a clear concept of how it will add value to managing the client's portfolio. Such a concept can be based on the manager's perception of an opportunity—or a problem—in the market that presents opportunities for this particular firm to increase the portfolio's rate of return.

In addition to a cogent concept of how to add value, the investment manager should have developed a sensible process for making decisions to *implement* that concept, and should have a valid record of achievement of the results intended.

Keep notes on the answers your investment manager gives to your questions. They can be brief but must be saved for future use—in comparing the answers you get at other times to the same or similar questions. This simple technique has been used for years—perhaps even for centuries—by the managers of the Scottish trusts.

The concept of using multiple managers has become increasingly popular among large clients in recent years. Several reasons are given:

1. The fund can select specialist managers skilled in each of several different kinds of investing wanted.
2. The fund can diversify against the risk of one manager's investment concept being out of tune with the overall market (as will surely happen from time to time).
3. Managers who fail to perform can be terminated more easily when they manage only part of the fund.

The problem with multiple managers is that the positive reasons become increasingly ephemeral as the number of managers increases. While it may be feasible to select one or two superior managers in a particular specialty, it's harder and harder to pick three or five or seven. There just aren't that many truly superior managers around.

While diversification does increase with each additional manager, when the separately managed portfolios are amalgamated into one fund and analyzed, it becomes clear that each additional manager adds less and less incremental diversification, but does incur higher and higher operating costs and fees, and moves closer and closer to the investment characteristics of the market fund.

Since market funds are readily available at low cost, the use of more and more different managers cannot be to reduce risk, because that can be accomplished more easily and more cheaply with a market fund.

Rationally, if the client is prepared to pay the higher fees inherent in multiple management, the objective must be to increase returns by finding managers who can find and exploit the occasional but significant opportunities that might arise from mispricing errors of other managers.

Realistically, important opportunities of this kind are only infrequently found. Therefore, the client might well force the manager to place all his bets on a very small number of decisions he believes are most attractive. If this forcing is not done, the client with multiple managers will most certainly be overpaying for excess diversification.

The argument that managers can be more easily terminated—with less harm to the fund and less harm to the management firm—if the account is relatively small to both parties is, of course, true. But it may be pernicious.

Clients might understandably be less careful in selecting or supervising managers they know they can terminate. And managers may be too cautious in asserting their best investment judgement if these clients might, during an interim period of adverse "performance," terminate them. Most investment managers believe, rightly or wrongly, that the tolerance of their clients for performance that differs significantly from the market and for portfolio decisions that differ from the conventional is least when needed most.

Consequently, unless guided by clearly defined investment objectives and policies, investment managers may be tempted to act as though their real goal is not to maximize investment results for their clients, but to maximize their probability of keeping the account. This could and does result in most portfolios being stuck in the "muddle of the middle," producing a high-cost but imperfect market portfolio.

Good clients will, if they decide to use active managers, insist that their managers adhere to the discipline of following through on agreed upon investment policy.

CONCLUSION

Clients—not their portfolio managers—have the most important job in successful investment management. Clients' central responsibilities are to decide on their long-term investment objectives and, with the expert advice of professional managers, determine a well-reasoned and realistic set of investment policies that can achieve the specified objectives of the client.

Only by separating responsibility for investment *policy* from responsibility for portfolio *operations* can a client delegate to a manager the authority to implement policy in daily portfolio operations without abdicating the client's responsibility for defining objectives and making sure that investment policies are designed to achieve the chosen objectives.

The great purpose of investment policy is to provide sound guidance to the portfolio manager, particularly when market conditions are most distressing and create the most urgent anxiety about the true wisdom of those policies.

Clients should study their total investment situation and their emotional tolerance of risk and the history of investment markets, because a mismatch between the market's sometimes grim realities and the financial and emotional needs of the investor can—and has—resulted in great harm.

Clients who study the realities of investing will be able to protect themselves and their investments from the conventional hope that they can find portfolio managers who will "beat the market." These clients will understand that the only way an active investment manager can beat the market is to find and exploit other investors' mistakes more often than they find and exploit his.

But so many investment managers are so very good at their work that they don't make enough mistakes, therefore, it is unlikely that any large institutional investor will be able to beat his professional competitors, either substantially or consistently. Most of the managers and clients who insist on trying will be disappointed by the results. It *is* a loser's game.

Happily, there is an easy way to win the loser's game by not playing—at least not playing by the conventional rules that are now out of date. As George Marshall counseled his senior officers on the way to winning World War II: "Don't fight the problem." Accept reality. Times have changed.

Even as the existing old ways of managing portfolios to beat the market have become obsolete, a new approach is now available—and works. It downplays portfolio operations, particularly of the heroic variety, and concentrates on carefully thought through, well-documented, and well-defined *policy.*

Recognizing that higher returns are the incentive and reward for investors taking—and sustaining—an above average market risk and that the highest returns therefore come from equity investments, clients should set their portfolios' asset mix at the highest ratio of equities that their economic and emotional limitations can afford and sustain.

To do their work well, clients must understand the turbulent nature of markets in the short term and the basic consistency of markets in the long term. This understanding will enable the effective client to increase his or her tolerance for interim market fluctuations and to concentrate on the long-term purpose of the portfolio, taking appropriate full advantage of any investor's greatest resource: time.

Soundly conceived, persistently followed long-term investment policy *is* the pathway to success in investing. The actions required are not complicated. The real challenge is to commit to the discipline of long-term investing and to avoid the compelling distractions of the excitement that surrounds, but is superfluous to, the real work of investing. This commitment to the discipline of long-term investing is the principal responsibility—and opportunity to contribute—of the *client.*

You now know all you will ever need to know to be truly successful with investments.

Index